# MICROSOFT AZURE

## ESSENTIAL USER GUIDE TO LEARN MICROSOFT AZURE

VOLUME 1

WILLIAM HAZELBERG

i

# TABLE OF CONTENTS

# INTRODUCTION

Microsoft Azure is Microsoft's cloud computing platform, providing a wide variety of services you can use without purchasing and provisioning your own hardware. Azure enables the rapid development of solutions and provides the resources to accomplish tasks that may not be feasible in an on-premises environment. Azure's compute, storage, network, and application services allow you to focus on building great solutions without the need to worry about how the physical infrastructure is assembled.

This book covers the fundamentals of Azure you need to start developing solutions right away. It concentrates on the features of the Azure platform that you are most likely to need to know rather than on every feature and service available on the platform. This book also provides several walkthroughs you can follow to learn how to create VMs and virtual networks, websites and storage accounts, and so on. In many cases, real-world tips are included to help you get the most out of your Azure experience.

In addition to its coverage of core Azure services, the book discusses common tools useful in creating and managing Azure-based solutions. The book wraps up by providing details on a few common business scenarios where Azure can provide compelling and valuable solutions, as well as a chapter providing overviews of some of the commonly used services not covered in the book.

## WHO SHOULD READ THIS BOOK

This book focuses on providing essential information about the key services of Azure for developers and IT professionals who are new to cloud computing. Detailed, step-by-step demonstrations are included to help the reader understand how to get started with each of the key services. This material is useful not only for those who have no prior experience with Azure, but also for those who need a refresher and those who may be familiar with one area but not others. Each chapter is standalone; there is no requirement that you perform the hands-on demonstrations from previous chapters to understand any particular chapter.

## ASSUMPTIONS

We expect that you have at least a minimal understanding of virtualized environments and virtual machines. There are no specific skills required overall for this book, but having some knowledge of the topic of each chapter will help you gain a deeper understanding. For example, the chapter on virtual networks will make more sense if you have some understanding of networking, and the chapter on databases will be more useful if you understand what a database is and why you might use one. Web development skills will provide a good background for understanding Azure Web Apps, and some understanding of identity will be helpful when studying the chapter on Active Directory.

## THIS BOOK MIGHT NOT BE FOR YOU IF...

This book might not be for you if you are looking for an in-depth developer or architecture-focused discussion on a wide range of Azure features, or if you are looking for details on other public or private cloud platforms.

## ORGANIZATION OF THIS BOOK

This book explores six foundational features of the Microsoft Azure platform, along with insights on getting started with Azure, management tools, and common business scenarios. This book also includes a chapter with overviews of some of the more commonly used services, such as HDInsight (Azure's Hadoop service) and Service Bus, but there are many services in the Azure platform that are not in the scope of this book, such as Azure Batch, Data Lake Analytics, and Azure DNS, just to mention a few. To learn about all of the services available in the Azure platform, start your journey at http://azure.microsoft.com. Also, there is a web application that shows the many services of Azure and allows you to drill down to learn move.

The topics explored in this book include:

* Getting started with Azure: Understand what cloud computing is, learn about Azure Resource Manager and Role-Based Access Control, visit the management portals, learn about billing, find out how you can contribute to the Azure documentation and code samples.

* Azure App Service and Web Apps: Learn about the Azure App Service, consisting of Web Apps, Logic Apps, Mobile Apps, API

Apps, and Function Apps. We will focus on Web Apps and how they work with the App Service and App Service plans, covering the topic from deployment to monitoring and scaling.

- Virtual Machines: Explore the basic features of Azure Virtual Machines, including how to create, configure, and manage them.

- Storage: Read about the basics of Azure Storage, including blobs, tables, queues, and file shares, as well as some of the options available such as Premium Storage and Cool Storage.

- Virtual Networks: Learn the basics of virtual networks, including how to create one, and why a virtual network might be necessary. This also covers site-to-site and point-to-site networking, as well as ExpressRoute.

- Databases: Explore two relational database options available in Azure: Azure SQL Database and SQL Server in Azure Virtual Machines.

- Azure Active Directory: Explore basic features of Azure AD, including creating a directory, users and groups, and using the application gallery.

- Management Tools: Explore three common tools for working with Azure: Visual Studio 2015 and the Azure SDK, Azure PowerShell cmdlets, and the Cross-Platform Command-Line Interface

- Additional Azure services: Get an overview about Azure services not covered in the book that may be fundamental to you now or in the future, such as Azure Service Fabric and Azure Container Service.

- Business Scenarios: Explore five common scenarios for utilizing Azure features: development and test, hybrid, application and infrastructure modernization, and Azure Mobile Apps, and Machine Learning.

## CONVENTIONS AND FEATURES IN THIS BOOK

This book presents information using conventions designed to make the information readable and easy to follow:

- To create specific Azure resources, follow the numbered steps listing each action you must take to complete the exercise.

- There are currently two management portals for Azure: the Azure portal at https://portal.azure.com and the Azure classic portal at http://manage.windowsazure.com. In most cases, the book uses the Azure portal, but the Azure classic portal may be used for those features that have not been migrated to the newer portal yet, such as Azure Active Directory.

- Boxed elements with labels such as "Note" or "See Also" provide additional information.

- A plus sign (+) between two key names means that you must press those keys at the same time. For example, "Press Alt+Tab" means that you hold down the Alt key while you press Tab.

- A right angle bracket between two or more menu items (e.g., File Browse > Virtual Machines) means that you should select the first menu or menu item, then the next,

# CHAPTER 1

# GETTING STARTED WITH MICROSOFT AZURE

The purpose of this ebook is to help you understand the fundamentals of Microsoft Azure so you can hit the ground running when you start using it. With an Azure account, you can work through the demos in this book and use them as hands-on labs. If you don't have an Azure account, you can sign up for a free trial at azure.microsoft.com. If you have an MSDN subscription, you can activate the included Azure benefits and use the associated monthly credit. You can also check out Purchase Options at https://azure.microsoft.com/pricing/purchase-options/ and Member Offers at https://azure.microsoft.com/pricing/member-offers/ (for members of MSDN, the Microsoft Partner Network, BizSpark, and other Microsoft programs).

## WHAT IS AZURE?

The following will give an overview of Azure, which is Microsoft's cloud computing platform.

## OVERVIEW OF CLOUD COMPUTING

Cloud computing provides a modern alternative to the traditional on-premises datacenter. A public cloud vendor is completely responsible for hardware purchase and maintenance and provides a wide variety of platform services that you can use. You lease whatever hardware and software services you require on an as-needed basis, thereby converting what had been a capital expense for hardware purchase into an operational expense. It also allows you to lease access to hardware and software resources that would be too expensive to purchase. Although you are limited to the hardware provided by the cloud vendor, you only have to pay for it when you use it.

Cloud environments provide an online portal experience, making it easy for users to manage compute, storage, network, and application resources. For example, in the Azure portal, a user can create a virtual machine (VM) configuration specifying the following: the VM size (with regard to CPU, RAM, and local disks), the operating system, any predeployed software, the network configuration, and the location of the VM. The user then can deploy the VM based on that configuration and within a few minutes access the deployed VM. This quick deployment compares favorably with the previous mechanism for deploying a physical machine, which could take weeks just for the procurement cycle.

In addition to the public cloud just described, there are private and hybrid clouds. In a private cloud, you create a cloud environment in your own datacenter and provide self-service access to compute resources to users in your organization. This offers a simulation of a public cloud to your users, but you remain completely responsible for the purchase and maintenance of the hardware and software services you provide. A hybrid cloud integrates public and private clouds, allowing you to host workloads in the most appropriate location. For example, you could host a high-scale website in the public cloud and link it to a highly secure database hosted in your private cloud (or on-premises datacenter).

Microsoft provides support for public, private, and hybrid clouds. Microsoft Azure, the focus of this book, is a public cloud. Microsoft Azure Stack is an add-on to Windows Server 2016 that allows you to deploy many core Azure services in your own datacenter and provides a self-service portal experience to your users. You can integrate these into a hybrid cloud through the use of a virtual private network.

## COMPARISON OF ON-PREMISES VERSUS AZURE

With an on-premises infrastructure, you have complete control over the hardware and software that you deploy. Historically, this has led to hardware procurement decisions focused on scaling up; that is, purchasing a server with more cores to satisfy a performance need. With Azure, you can deploy only the hardware provided by Microsoft. This leads to a focus on scale-out through the deployment of additional compute nodes to satisfy a performance need. Although this has consequences for the design of an appropriate software architecture, there is now ample proof that the scale-out of commodity hardware is significantly more cost-effective than scale-up through expensive hardware.

Microsoft has deployed Azure datacenters in over 22 regions around the globe from Melbourne to Amsterdam and Sao Paulo to Singapore.

Additionally, Microsoft has an arrangement with 21Vianet, making Azure available in two regions in China. Microsoft has also announced the deployment of Azure to another eight regions. Only the largest global enterprises are able to deploy datacenters in this manner, so using Azure makes it easy for enterprises of any size to deploy their services close to their customers, wherever they are in the world. And you can do that without ever leaving your office.

For startups, Azure allows you to start with very low cost and scale rapidly as you gain customers. You would not face a large up-front capital investment to create a new VM—or even several new VMs. The use of cloud computing fits well with the scale fast, fail fast model of startup growth.

Azure provides the flexibility to set up development and test configurations quickly. These deployments can be scripted, giving you the ability to spin up a development or test environment, do the testing, and spin it back down. This keeps the cost very low, and maintenance is almost nonexistent.

Another advantage of Azure is that you can try new versions of software without having to upgrade on-premises equipment. For example, if you want to see the ramifications of running your application against Microsoft SQL Server 2016 instead of Microsoft SQL Server 2014, you can create a SQL Server 2016 instance and run a copy of your services against the new database, all without having to allocate hardware and run wires. Or you can run on a VM with Microsoft Windows Server 2012 R2 instead of Microsoft Windows Server 2008 R2.

## CLOUD OFFERING

Cloud computing usually is classified in three categories: SaaS, PaaS, and IaaS. However, as the cloud matures, the distinction among these is being eroded.

## SAAS: SOFTWARE AS A SERVICE

SaaS is software that is centrally hosted and managed for the end customer. It usually is based on a multitenant architecture—a single version of the application is used for all customers. It can be scaled out to multiple instances to ensure the best performance in all locations. SaaS software typically is licensed through a monthly or annual subscription.

Microsoft Office 365 is a prototypical model of a SaaS offering. Subscribers pay a monthly or annual subscription fee, and they get Exchange as a Service (online and/or desktop Outlook), Storage as a Service (OneDrive), and the rest of the Microsoft Office Suite (online, the desktop version, or both).

Subscribers are always provided the most recent version. This essentially allows you to have a

Microsoft Exchange server without having to purchase a server and install and support Exchange—the Exchange server is managed for you, including software patches and updates. Compared to installing and upgrading Office every year, this is much less expensive and requires much less effort to keep updated.

Other examples of SaaS include Dropbox, WordPress, and Amazon Kindle.

## PAAS: PLATFORM AS A SERVICE

With PaaS, you deploy your application into an application-hosting environment provided by the cloud service vendor. The developer provides the application, and the PaaS vendor provides the ability to deploy and run it. This frees developers from infrastructure management, allowing them to focus strictly on development.

Azure provides several PaaS compute offerings, including the Web Apps feature in Azure App Service and Azure Cloud Services (web and worker roles). In either case, developers have multiple ways to deploy their application without knowing anything about the nuts and bolts supporting it. Developers don't have to create VMs, use Remote Desktop Protocol (RDP) to log into each one, and install the application. They just hit a button (or pretty close to it), and the tools provided by Microsoft provision the VMs and then deploy and install the application on them.

## IAAS: INFRASTRUCTURE AS A SERVICE

An IaaS cloud vendor runs and manages server farms running virtualization software, enabling you to create VMs that run on the vendor's infrastructure. Depending on the vendor, you can create a VM running Windows or Linux and install anything you want on it. Azure provides the ability to set up virtual networks, load balancers, and storage and to use many other services that run on its infrastructure. You don't have control over the hardware or virtualization software, but you do have control over almost everything else. In fact, unlike PaaS, you are completely responsible for it.

Azure Virtual Machines, the Azure IaaS offering, is a popular choice when migrating services to Azure because it enables the "lift and shift" model for migration. You can configure a VM similar to the infrastructure currently running your services in your datacenter and migrate your software to the new VM. You might need to make tweaks, such as URLs to other services or storage, but many applications can be migrated in this manner.

Azure VM Scale Sets (VMSS) is built on top of Azure Virtual Machines and provides an easy way to deploy clusters of identical VMs. VMSS also supports autoscaling so that new VMs can be deployed automatically when required. This makes VMSS an ideal platform to host higher-level microservice compute clusters such as for Azure Service Fabric and the Azure Container Service.

## AZURE SERVICES

Azure includes many services in its cloud computing platform. Let's talk about a few of them.

- Compute services This includes the Azure Virtual Machines—both Linux and Windows, Cloud Services, App Services (Web Apps, Mobile Apps, Logic Apps, API Apps, and Function Apps), Batch (for large-scale parallel and batch compute jobs), RemoteApp, Service Fabric, and the Azure Container Service.

- Data services This includes Microsoft Azure Storage (comprised of the Blob, Queue, Table, and Azure Files services), Azure SQL Database, DocumentDB, StorSimple, and the Redis Cache.

- Application services This includes services that you can use to help build and operate your applications, such as Azure Active Directory (Azure AD), Service Bus for connecting distributed systems, HDInsight for processing big data, Azure Scheduler, and Azure Media Services.

- Network services This includes Azure features such as Virtual Networks, ExpressRoute, Azure DNS, Azure Traffic Manager, and the Azure Content Delivery Network.

When migrating an application, it is worthwhile to have some understanding of the different services available in Azure because you might be able to use them to simplify the migration of your application and improve its robustness.

# THE NEW WORLD: AZURE RESOURCE MANAGER

The Azure Resource Manager is the new methodology for deploying resources.

## WHAT IS IT?

Since it went into public preview, the Azure Service Management (ASM) deployment model has been used to deploy services. In the Azure portal, services managed with ASM are referred to as *classic*. In 2015, Microsoft introduced the Resource Manager deployment model as a modern, more functional replacement for ASM. The Resource Manager deployment model is recommended for all new Azure workloads.

These deployment models are often referred to as *control planes* because they are used to control services, not just to deploy them. This is different from a data plane, which manages the data used by a service.

Typically, your running Azure infrastructure will contain many resources, but some of the resources will be related to one another in some way, such as all being the component services required to run a web application. For example, you might have two VMs running the web application, using a database to store data, and residing in the same virtual network. With Resource Manager, you deploy these assets into the same resource group and manage and monitor them together. You can deploy, update, or delete all of the resources in a resource group in one operation.

In this example, the resource group would contain the following:

* VM1

* VM2

* Virtual network

* Storage account

* Azure SQL Database

You can also create a template that precisely defines all the Resource Manager resources in a deployment. You can then deploy this Resource Manager template into a resource group as a single control-plane operation, with Resource Manager in Azure ensuring that resources are deployed correctly. After deployment, Resource Manager provides security, auditing, and tagging features to help you manage your resources.

## WHY USE RESOURCE MANAGER?

There are several advantages to using Resource Manager. The deployment is faster because resources can be deployed in parallel rather than sequentially as they are in ASM. The Resource Manager model enables each service to have its own service provider, and they can update it as needed independently of the other services. Azure Storage has its own service provider, VMs have their own service provider, and so on. With the ASM model, all services had to be updated at one time, so if one service was finished and the rest were not, the one that was ready had to wait on the others before it could be released. Here are some of the other major advantages to the Resource Manager model:

- Deployment using templates

- You can create a reusable (JSON) template that can be used to deploy all of the resources for a specific solution in one fell swoop. You no longer have to create a VM in the portal, wait for it to finish, then create the next VM, and so on.

- You can use the template to redeploy the same resources repeatedly. For example, you may set up the resources in a test environment and find that it doesn't fit your needs. You can delete the resource group, which removes all of the resources for you, then tweak your template and try again. If you only want to make changes to the resources deployed, you can just change the template and deploy it again, and Resource Manager will change the resources to conform to the new template.

- You can take that template and easily re-create multiple versions of your infrastructure, such as staging and production. You can parameterize fields such as the VM name, network name, storage account name, etc., and load the template repeatedly, using different parameters.

- Resource Manager can identify dependencies in a template but allows you to specify additional dependencies if necessary. For example, you wouldn't want to deploy a virtual machine before creating the storage account for the VHD files that are used for the OS and data disks.

- Security

- You can use the new Role-Based Access Control (RBAC) to control access to the resources in the group. For example, you can assign the Owner role to a user, giving that user full administrative privileges to those resources in the group but not to other resources in the subscription. Other roles include Reader (you can read anything except secrets) and Contributor (you can do most anything except add or revoke access).

- Billing

- To help organize all of the resources in a subscription for billing purposes, you can assign tags to each resource and then retrieve all of the billing information for a specific tag.

  For example, if one department owns a web application and several related components, you can assign the same tag to all of those resources. Then, you can retrieve the billing for that department by retrieving the billing for that tag.

Note If you apply a tag to a resource group, the resources in the group do not inherit that tag. You have to apply the tag to each individual resource.

## MAXIMIZE THE BENEFITS OF USING RESOURCE MANAGER

Microsoft has several suggestions to help you maximize the use of the Resource Manager model when working with your applications and components.

- Use templates rather than using scripting like PowerShell or the Azure Command-Line Interface (CLI). Using a template allows resources to be deployed in parallel, making it much faster than using a script executed sequentially.

- Automate as much as possible by leveraging templates. You can include configurations for various extensions like PowerShell DSC and Web Deploy. This way, you don't need any manual steps to create and configure the resources.

- Use PowerShell or the Azure CLI to manage the resources, such as to start or stop a virtual machine or application.

- Put resources with the same lifecycle in the same resource group. In our example above, what if the database is used by multiple applications? If that's true, or if the database is going to live on even after the application is retired or removed, you don't want to re-create the database every time you redeploy the application and its components. In that case, put the database in its own resource group.

## RESOURCE GROUP TIPS

You can decide how to allocate your resources to resource groups based on what makes sense for you and your organization. A resource group is a logical container to hold related resources for an application or group of applications. These tips should be considered when making decisions about your resource group:

• As noted before, all of the resources in a group should have the same lifecycle.

• A resource can only be assigned to one group at a time.

• A resource can be added to or removed from a resource group at any time. Note that every resource must belong to a resource group, so if you remove it from one group, you have to add it to another.

• Most types of resource can be moved to a different resource group at any time.

• The resources in a resource group can be in different regions.

• You can use a resource group to control access for the resources therein.

## TIPS FOR USING RESOURCE MANAGER TEMPLATES

Resource Manager templates define the deployment and configuration of your application. They are used to deploy an application and all of its component resources repeatedly.

You can divide the deployments in a set of templates and create a master template that links in all of the required templates.

Templates can be modified and redeployed with updates. For example, you can add a new resource or update configuration information about a resource in a template. When deployed again, Resource Manager will create any new resources it finds and perform updates for any that have been changed. Then, you add a third subnet and redeploy the template, and you can see the third subnet appear in the Azure portal.

Templates can be parameterized to allow you more flexibility in deployment. This is what allows you to use the same template repeatedly but with different values, such as VM name, virtual network name, storage account name, region, and so on.

You can export the current state of the resources in a resource group to a template. This can then be used as a pattern for other deployments, or it can be edited and redeployed to make changes and additions to the current resource group's resources.

Here is an example of a JSON template. Deploying this template will create a storage account in West US called mystorage. This is parameterized; you can include a parameter file that provides the values for newStorageAccountName and location. Otherwise, it will use the defaults.

```
{
  "$schema":
"http://schema.management.azure.com/schemas/2015-01-
01/deploymentTemplate.json#",
  "contentVersion": "1.0.0.0",
  "parameters": {
   "newStorageaccountName": {
     "type": "string",
     "defaultValue": "mystorage",
     "metadata": {
       "description": "Unique DNS Name for the Storage account
where the Virtual Machine's disks will be placed."
     }
   },

   "location": {
     "type": "string",
     "defaultValue": "West US",
     "allowedValues": [
       "West US",
       "East US"
     ],
     "metadata": {
       "description": "Restricts choices to where premium storage is
located in the US."
     }
   }
  },

  "resources": [
   {
     "type": "Microsoft.Storage/storageaccounts",
     "name": "[parameters('newStorageaccountName')]",
     "apiVersion": "2015-06-15",
```

```
      "location": "[parameters('location')]",
      "properties": {
        "accountType": "Standard_LRS"
      }
     }
    ]
}
```

# THE CLASSIC DEPLOYMENT MODEL

Let's talk a bit about what came before Resource Manager. These resources are now referred to as *classic*. For example, you can have storage accounts, virtual machines, and virtual networks that use the classic deployment model. The classic and Resource Manager models are not compatible with each other. The classic resources cannot be seen by the Resource Manager resources, and vice versa. For example, the PaaS Cloud Services feature of Azure is a classic feature, so you can only use it with storage accounts that are classic storage accounts. The exception to that rule is that you can use classic storage accounts to host Resource Manager VMs. This will make it easier to migrate your VMs from the classic deployment model to the Resource Manager deployment model.

Note that this means you may log into the classic Azure portal and see classic resources but not see Resource Manager resources, and vice versa.

Note There are two versions of the portal. The production portal is the Azure portal at https://portal.azure.com. Most features have been moved to the Azure portal, with some exceptions such as Azure Active Directory (Azure AD). The previous portal is called the classic Azure portal (https://manage.windowsazure.com), and it can still be used to manage Azure AD and to configure and scale classic resources such as Cloud Services.

You can migrate your assets from the classic to the Resource Manager deployment model.

*   For storage accounts, you can use AzCopy to copy blobs, files, and tables to a new Resource Manager storage account. Note that tables must be exported from the classic account and then imported into the Resource Manager account.

*   For virtual machines, you can shut them down and copy their VHD file to a new Resource Manager storage account and then use the VHD file to re-create the VM.

- For virtual networks, you can re-create them as Resource Manager VNets.

- There is also a migration service that is in public preview. Microsoft recommends using this only for nonproduction workloads at this time

## POWERSHELL CHANGES FOR THE RESOURCE MANAGER AND CLASSIC DEPLOYMENT MODELS

One of the other changes made when the Azure team created the Resource Manager model was to create PowerShell cmdlets that work just for the Resource Manager model. They did this by appending "Rm" to "Azure" in the name of the cmdlets. For example, to create a classic storage account, you would use the *New-AzureStorageAccount* cmdlet. To create a Resource Manager storage account, you would use the *New-AzureRmStorageAccount* cmdlet.

Microsoft did this so you could easily tell which kind of resource you were creating. Also, this ensures that scripts that are currently being used will continue to work. Each time you deploy a Resource Manager resource, you have to specify the resource group into which it should be placed. Also, some of the cmdlets for Resource Manager (such as creating a VM) have more details than their counterparts in the classic model.

One last note: for storage accounts, the only PowerShell cmdlets impacted are on the control plane, such as those for creating a storage account, listing storage accounts, removing a storage account, and so on. All of the PowerShell cmdlets used to access the actual objects in storage—blobs, tables, queues, and files—remain unchanged. So once you are pointed to the right storage account, you're good to go.

## ROLE-BASED ACCESS CONTROL

In this section, we'll take a look at Role-Based Access Control (RBAC) to understand how you can use it to manage the security for your Resource Manager resources.

# WHAT IS IT?

In addition to the Resource Manager deployment model that allows you to group and manage your related resources, Microsoft introduced RBAC, providing fine-grained control over the operations and scope with which a user can perform a control-plant action. The previous methodology (classic) only allows you to grant either full administrative privileges to everything in a subscription or no access at all.

With Resource Manager, you can grant permissions at a specified scope: subscription, resource group, or resource. This means you can deploy a set of resources into a resource group and then grant permissions to one or more specific users, groups, or service principal. Those users will only have the permissions granted to those resources in that resource group. This access does not allow them to modify resources in other resource groups. You can also give a user permission to manage a single VM, and that's all that user will be able to access and administer.

In addition to users, Azure RBAC also supports service principals that formally are identities representing applications, but informally are used by RBAC to allow automated processes to manage Resource Manager resources. To grant access, you assign a role to the user, group, or service principal. There are many predefined roles, and you can also define your own custom roles.

# ROLES

Each role has a list of Actions and Not Actions. The Actions are allowed, and the Not Actions are excluded. For example, there is a role called Contributor. With this role, a user can manage everything except access. This role has the following Actions and Not Actions:

- Actions: * > Can create and manage resources of all types

- Not Action: Microsoft.Authorization/*/Write > Can't create roles

  or assign roles > Not Action: Microsoft.Authorization/*/Delete >

  Can't delete roles or role assignments

Let's take a look at some of the most common roles.

- Owner A user with this role can manage everything, including access. This role has no Not Actions. This is synonymous with Co-Administrator in the classic deployment model.

- Reader A user with this role can read resources of all types (except secrets) but can't make changes. This role will allow someone to look at the properties of a storage account, but it won't let that person retrieve the access keys.

- SQL DB Contributor A user with this role can manage SQL databases but not their securityrelated policies.

- SQL Security Manager A user with this role can manage the security-related policies of SQL Servers and databases.

- Storage Account Contributor A user with this role can manage storage accounts but cannot manage access to the storage accounts. This means the user with this role can't assign any roles to any users for the storage account. Note that the user with this role *can* retrieve the access keys for the storage account, which means they have full access to the data in the storage account.

- Virtual Machine Contributor A user with this role can manage virtual machines but can't manage the VNet to which they are connected or the storage account where the VHD file resides. Note that this role *does* include access to the storage account keys, which is needed to create the container for the VHD files as well as the VHD files themselves.

These are only a few of the many roles that can be assigned to a user, a group of users, or an application.

## CUSTOM ROLES

If none of the built-in roles and no combination of the built-in roles provides exactly what you need, you can create a custom role. You can do this using PowerShell, the Azure CLI, or the REST APIs. Once you create a custom role, you can assign it to a user, group, or application for a subscription, resource group, or resource. Custom roles are stored in the Azure AD and can be shared across all subscriptions that use the same Active Directory.

For example, you could create a custom role for monitoring and restarting virtual machines. Here are the Actions you would assign to that role:

- Microsoft.Storage/*/read

- Microsoft.Network/*/read

- Microsoft.Compute/*/read

- Microsoft.Compute/virtualMachines;/start/action
- Microsoft.Compute/virtualMachines/restart/action
- Microsoft.Authorization/*/read
- Microsoft.Resources/subscriptions/resourceGroups/read
- Microsoft.Insights/alertRules/*
- Microsoft.Insights/diagnosticSettings/*
- Microsoft.Support/*

Note that as requested, this role can only start and restart virtual machines. It can't create them or delete them.

A convenient way to create a custom role is to download the definition of an existing role and use that as a starting point. When you create a custom role, you also need to specify in which subscriptions it can be used—at least one must be specified.

In the next section, we'll see how to assign roles to users for a resource group and how to give full administrative privileges for a subscription to a user.

## THE AZURE PORTAL

An online management portal provides the easiest way to manage the resources you deploy into Azure. You can use this to create virtual networks, set up Web Apps, create VMs, define storage accounts, and so on, as listed in the previous section.

As noted earlier in this chapter, there are currently two versions of the portal. The production portal is the Azure portal at https://portal.azure.com. Most features have been moved to the Azure portal, with some exceptions such as Azure AD. The previous portal is called the classic Azure portal

(https://manage.windowsazure.com), and it can still be used to manage Azure AD and to configure and scale classic resources such as Cloud Services.

In most cases, you will be using the Azure portal, so that's what we're going to focus on in this book. All of the resources that use the Resource Manager deployment model can only be accessed in the Azure portal.

Let's take a look at the Azure portal and how you navigate through it.

# DASHBOARD AND HUB

The Azure portal is located at https://portal.azure.com. When you open this the first time, it will look similar to Figure 1-1.

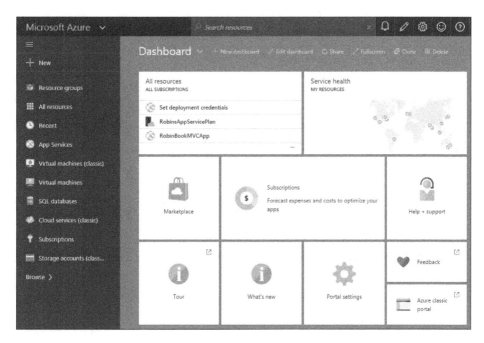

Figure 1-1 Azure portal.

This is called your Dashboard. The column on the left is called a hub; it shows you a core set of options such as Resource Groups, All Resources, and Recent. The other items on this hub are resources you have selected and/or used before. For example, I have recently created some App Services and VMs. You can click any of these, and it will show the resources you have for that type. For example, if you click SQL Databases, it will show a list of your SQL Databases.

You can customize the list of resources that show up in that left hub. If you click Browse, you will see a selection screen showing all of the options, and you can select which ones you want to appear, as displayed in Figure 1-2.

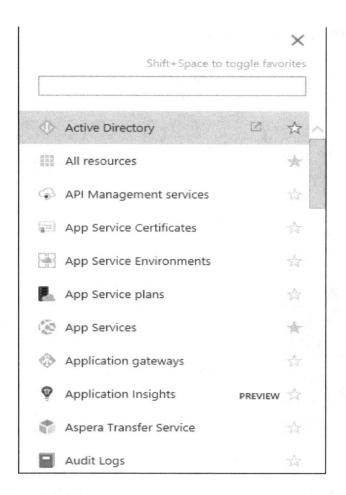

Figure 1-2 Configure default hub in the Azure portal.

The area on the right with the tiles is called your Dashboard. You can customize this by adding tiles, removing tiles, resizing tiles, and so on by selecting Edit Dashboard, as shown in Figure 1-3.

Figure 1-3 How to edit the Dashboard in the Azure portal.

As you create resources, you can choose to pin them to the Dashboard, and it will add them to this section.

There are a couple of default tiles on the Dashboard that are of interest.

- All Resources Clicking this will bring up a list of all of your resources.

- Service Health This shows the health of the regions around the world. If you click this, it will show a list of the regions, and you can select one to get more detailed information.

- Marketplace This will take you directly to the Marketplace blade where you can search for and add resources.

- Subscriptions This shows the subscriptions that can be managed by the account you are using. You can select a subscription and see the billing information for the current month. If you have a starting credit, this will show the amount of credit left. Accounts having starting credit include MSDN accounts and BizSpark accounts.

- Help + Support This takes you to the blade where you can submit a new support request and manage the requests you have already put in. It also provides links to the MSDN forums and StackOverflow where you can post questions.

Now, let's look at the icons in the upper-right corner of the Azure portal, as shown in Figure 1-4.

Figure 1-4 Notifications, settings, etc. in the Azure portal.

From left to right, here's what these icons mean:

- Clicking the bell shows notifications from this session. For example, if you create a new VM, when it's finished, it will put a notification here.

- Clicking the pencil puts the Dashboard into edit mode, just like clicking Edit Dashboard above.

- Clicking the gear icon brings up the Settings screen for the portal, where you can do things like enable or disable toast notifications, set the default language, and so on.

- Clicking the smiley face will show a dialog you can use to send feedback to the portal team.

- Clicking the question mark will show a drop-down menu allowing you to create a new support request, view your current support requests, and so on.

- The last field shows the account you have used to log into the portal. If you administer more than one subscription, this will show the list of Azure ADs to which the user belongs. You can click this to sign out, change your password, or submit an idea.

## CREATING AND VIEWING RESOURCES

As you make selections, the portal scrolls to the right. The separate sections that get opened are called blades.

Click New in the main hub. You see a categorized list of the resources available, as shown in Figure 15. This is a new blade.

Figure 1-5 Creating a new resource in the Azure portal

If you click See All, it will take you to the Azure Marketplace. The Marketplace contains all of the resources that you can use in Azure. This includes everything from VM images, which are certified before being made available, all of the SQL Server options, and Web Apps. It also includes applications such as Drupal and WordPress. To add any resource, you can search for it, then select it to add it to your Azure subscription.

You can also select a category on this blade. It will show the list of resources valid for that category, and you can then select which one you want to create. For example, to create a VM, you would click the Virtual Machines category; to create a storage account or a SQL Server, you would click Data + Storage.

Once you have created some resources, there are several ways to view them. Let's look back in the main hub (Figure 1-1), which has two helpful options—Resource Groups and All Resources.

## VIEW BY RESOURCE GROUP

Use this option to see all of your resources by resource group. Click Resource Groups, and you see a blade like Figure 1-6 showing all of your resource groups.

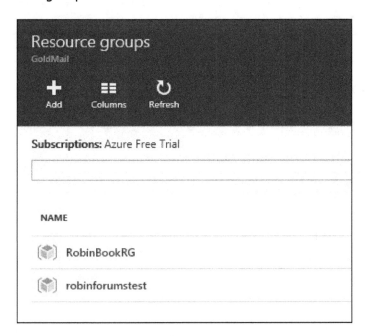

Figure 1-6 Screenshot showing all of your resource groups in the Azure portal.

Next, select one of the resource groups, and it shows all of the resources deployed to that group (Figure 1-7).

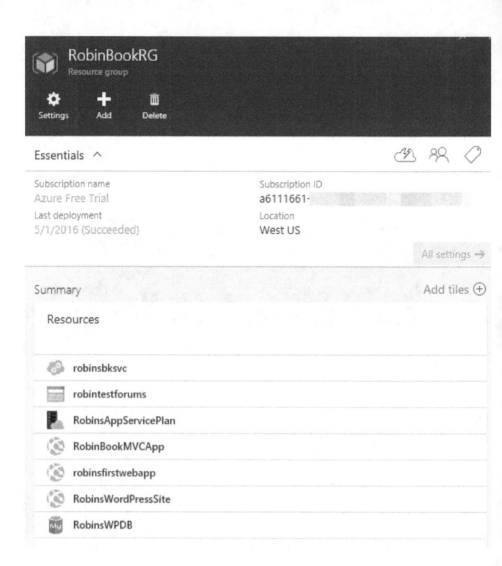

Figure 1-7 List of resources in the selected resource group.

You can click any of the resources here, and they will be displayed in a new blade.

Click All Settings to show the Settings blade (Figure 1-8). From there, you can look at the costs by resource, view the deployment history of the resources, set tags and locks, and manage what users have access to this resource group.

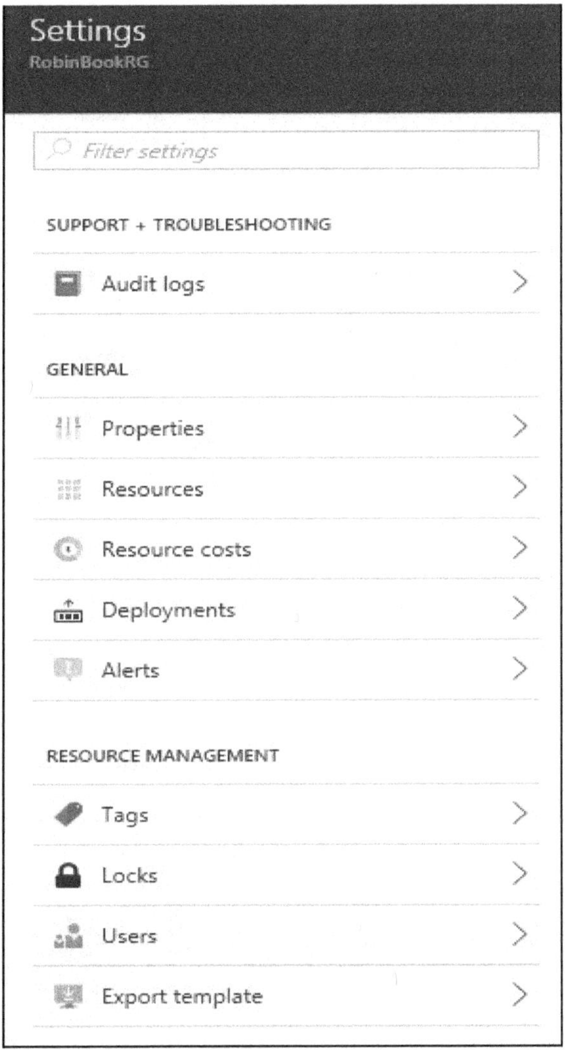

Figure 1-8 Settings blade when looking at resources in a resource group.

This is where you can use RBAC to control access to all of the resources in the same resource group at one time by assigning roles to users. The user has to be set up in the Azure AD, which is done in the classic Azure portal (https://manage.windowsazure.com).

Let's give VM Contributor access to another user account. This is granting the ability to manage the VMs but not the ability to manage the access to the VMs. So this new user could not grant access to anybody else. If you want someone to have full administrative

27

privileges of all the resources in the resource group, you can grant that user the Owner role.

In the Users blade, click Add. You are prompted to select the role you want the user to have (Figure 1-

9).

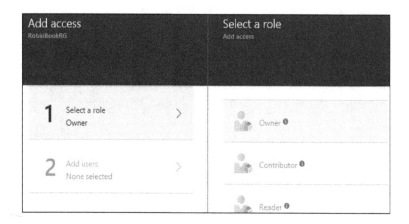

Figure 1-9 Select a role to assign to a new user.

Look through the list and find the Virtual Machine Contributor role and select it. The Add Access blade highlights Add Users and shows a list of users to the right from which to select (Figure 1-10). Select an account and then click Select at the bottom of the blade.

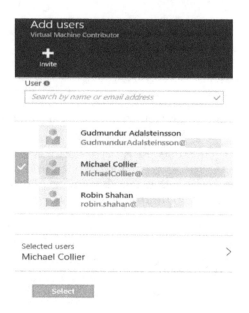

Figure 1-10 Select a user to add.

Next, click OK on the Add Access blade. It returns to the Users screen, which now reflects the user(s) added and their roles (Figure 1-11).

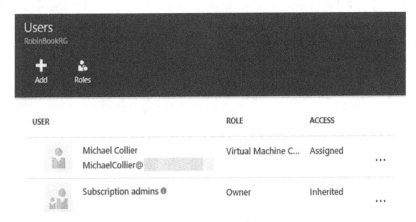

Figure 1-11 List of users and assigned roles.

I added the Virtual Machine Contributor role for Michael Collier. This means that Michael Collier now has the ability to manage the VMs in that resource group.

## VIEW BY RESOURCE

Back in the main hub (Figure 1-1), let's look at the other view of our resources. Click All Resources. This shows exactly what you expect—a list of all your resources (Figure 1-12). You can edit the columns by selecting Columns. I've added the Type column because I can never remember what all of the icons mean.

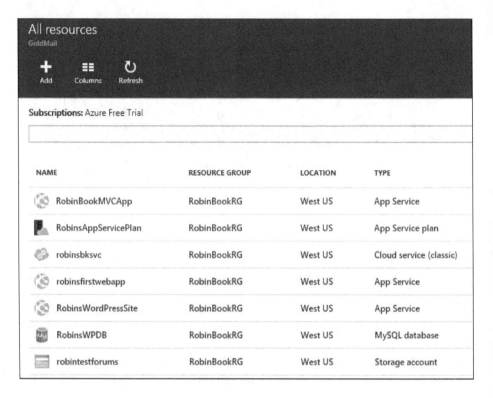

Figure 1-12 List of resources in the subscription.

Clicking any resource brings up a blade for that specific resource.

## SUBSCRIPTION MANAGEMENT AND BILLING

In this section, we'll look at the subscription types available and how to manage access to your subscription, as well as how to check your current billing balance.

## AVAILABLE SUBSCRIPTIONS

There are several different kinds of subscriptions providing access to Azure services. You must have a Microsoft account (created by you for personal use) or a work or school account (issued by an administrator for business or academic use) to access these subscriptions.

Let's take a look at the most common subscriptions:

- Free accounts The link to sign up for a free account is on the front page of azure.com. This gives you a $200 credit over the course of 30 days to try out any combination of resources in Azure. If you exceed your credit amount, your account will be suspended. At the end of the trial, your services will be decommissioned and will no longer work. You can upgrade this to a pay-asyou-go subscription at any time.

- MSDN subscriptions If you have an MSDN subscription, you get a specific amount in Azure credit each month. For example, if you have a Visual Studio Enterprise with MSDN subscription, you get $150 per month in Azure credit.

  If you exceed the credit amount, your service will be disabled until the next month starts. You can turn off the spending limit and add a credit card to be used for the additional costs. Some of these costs are discounted for MSDN accounts. For example, you pay the Linux price for VMs running Windows Server, and there is no additional charge for Microsoft Servers such as Microsoft SQL Server. This makes MSDN accounts ideal for development and test scenarios.

  For more information and to see the available MSDN subscription tiers, check out http://azure.microsoft.com/pricing/member-offers/msdn-benefits-details/. Note that these subscriptions are to be used for development and testing, not for production.

- BizSpark accounts The BizSpark program provides a lot of benefits to startups, not the least of which is access to all of Microsoft's software for development and test environments for up to five MSDN accounts. In addition to these benefits, you get $150 in Azure credit for each of those five MSDN accounts, and you pay reduced rates for several of the Azure services, such as Windows Virtual Machines.

  For more information, check out http://azure.microsoft.com/offers/ms-azr-0064p/.

- Pay-as-you-go With this subscription, you pay for what you use by attaching a credit card or debit card to the account. If you are an organization, you can also be approved for invoicing.

  For more information, check out http://azure.microsoft.com/offers/ms-azr-0003p/.

- Enterprise agreements With an enterprise agreement, you commit to using a certain amount of services in Azure over the next year, and you pay that amount ahead of time. The commitment that you make is consumed throughout the year. If you exceed the commitment amount, you can pay the overage in arrears. Depending on the amount of the commitment, you get a discount on the services in Azure.

For more information, check out http://azure.microsoft.com/pricing/enterprise-agreement/.

## SHARE ADMINISTRATIVE PRIVILEGES FOR YOUR AZURE SUBSCRIPTION

Once you have signed up for an Azure subscription, you can give administrative access to additional Microsoft accounts. This is done differently depending on whether you are using the classic Azure portal or the Azure portal. If you want the new account to be able to administer the subscription in both portals, you must make sure it has been given access in each portal. You want to do this if you need someone to administer the Azure AD for the subscription or if the subscription contains classic resources.

As we discussed previously, the Azure portal uses RBAC, and the classic Azure portal does not. This means in the classic Azure portal, you can *only* grant full administrative (co-admin) access to an account.

## ADD ADMINISTRATIVE PRIVILEGES IN THE AZURE PORTAL

We just saw how to grant administrative privileges to a resource group in the Azure portal. Granting administrative privileges is almost the same process, except instead of selecting a resource group, you select the subscription.

Go to the hub (the selector on the far left) and select Subscriptions, then select the Subscription to which you want to add an administrator. Click Settings to go to the Settings blade, and then select Users.

From the Users blade, you can use the same process we used before. Click Add, select the Owner role this time, select the user to whom you want to grant this role, and click OK to add the user to the RBAC settings for the subscription. They will show up in the Users blade with the user's new permission.

If you want to grant access to one specific resource, you can select the resource from the All Resources blade, go to Settings > Users, and add a user and role exactly the same way.

## GRANTING ADMINISTRATIVE PRIVILEGES IN THE CLASSIC AZURE PORTAL

To grant administrative access to an account in the classic Azure portal, add the user's account as a co-administrator to the subscription. This account will have all of the same privileges as the owner of the original subscription, but it does not allow the user to change the service administrator or to add and remove other co-administrators.

By using the classic Azure portal with administrative access, the user can access and maintain classic resources, such as classic storage accounts. There are also some Resource Manager resources that the account can impact, such as Web Apps. However, this user can't see storage accounts and virtual machines created with the Resource Manager deployment model.

Note that co-administrators are automatically added to the Subscription Admin RBAC role.

## PRICING CALCULATOR

Pricing for your Azure infrastructure can be estimated by using the pricing calculator found at http://azure.microsoft.com/pricing/calculator/ (Figure 1-13).

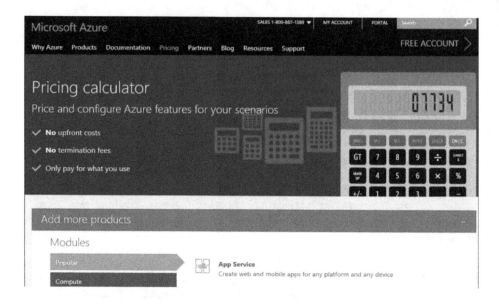

Figure 1-13 The pricing calculator.

The pricing for each service in Azure is different. Many Azure services provide Basic, Standard, and Premium tiers, usually with several price and performance levels in each tier, allowing you to select an appropriate performance level for your use of the service. As you change the selections, the pricing estimate is provided on the right side of the page. You can look at each feature separately or select several resources to estimate multiple features together.

Let's create a pricing example for two virtual machines and a storage account with 500 GB of data.

1. Click Compute > Virtual Machines. A message appears saying it has been added.

2. Click Data & Storage > Storage. A message appears saying it has been added.

3. Now, scroll to the bottom of the page, and you see it has added Virtual Machines and Storage. It also shows the total for all the resources you've specified.

4. On the Virtual Machines tile, set the Region to the one closest to you and set Type to Windows (other options include Linux). Next, set the Pricing Tier to Standard. Then, check the drop-down list on instance size and select a D2 V2. If we set the storage to Premium storage, this will also work for DS2 V2 VMs because the pricing is identical for D2 and DS2 VMs. D2 VMs use Standard storage; DS2 VMs use Premium storage.

34

Next, set the number of virtual machines to 2 (Figure 1-14)

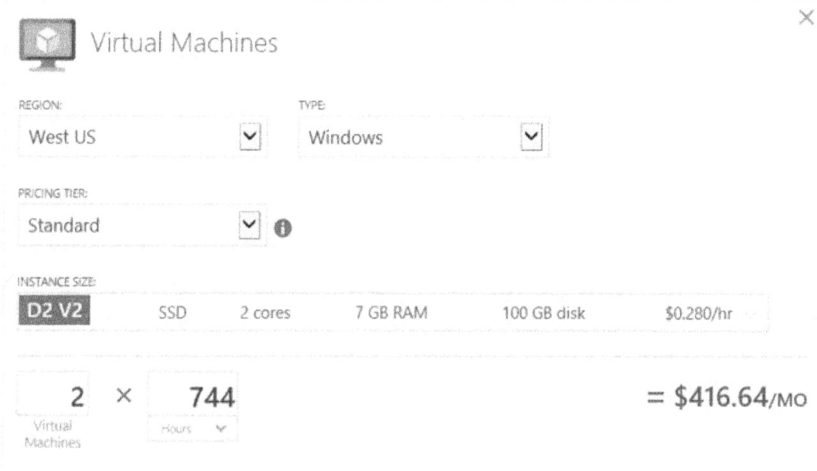

Figure 1-14 Calculating pricing on two virtual machines.

This shows an estimated cost for having those two virtual machines.

On the Storage tile, set the Region. Set Type to Page Blob and Disk, indicating that we are going to use this storage account to store the VHD files for our virtual machines. Set the Pricing Tier to Premium (SSD). Select the P30 disk. If you are deploying VMs, you want to use Premium storage for the best reliability and speed; Premium storage only uses SSDs. This will give an estimated cost for that configuration (Figure 1-15).

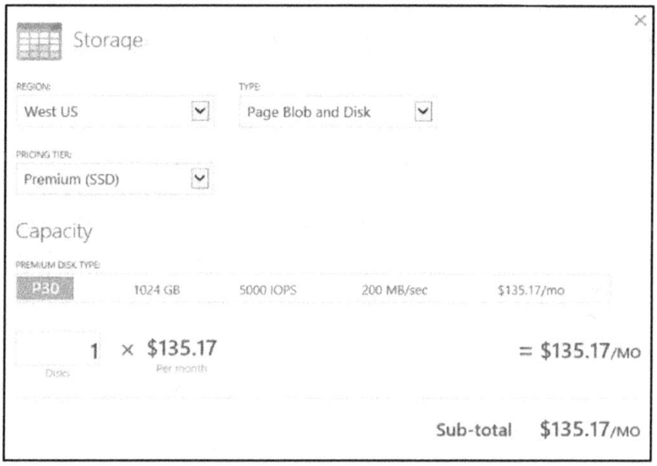

Figure 1-15 Calculating price on storage.

5. Now if you look at the total section, it gives a total estimated cost for the two virtual machines and the storage (Figure 1-16).

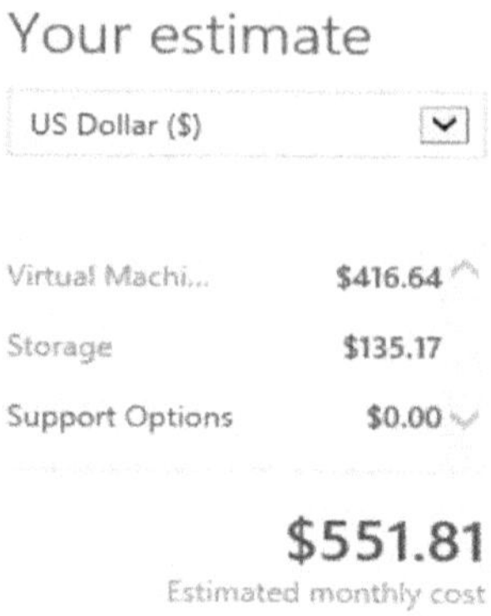

## Your estimate

US Dollar ($)

| | |
|---|---|
| Virtual Machi... | $416.64 |
| Storage | $135.17 |
| Support Options | $0.00 |

### $551.81
Estimated monthly cost

Figure 1-16 Calculating total cost of selected resources.

6. If you click Export Estimate, it will export all of the data to an Excel spreadsheet.

The pricing calculator can be helpful in estimating your Azure costs for new projects you want to add or for an entire infrastructure design.

> Note The overall pricing plan page does not include variations by region, but you can find those if you go to the individual service pricing pages at http://azure.microsoft.com/pricing/ and select the service in which you're interested. At that point, you can also select the specific region.

## VIEWING BILLING IN THE AZURE PORTAL

An important component of using Azure is being able to view your billing information. If you have an account that allows you a certain amount of credit, it's nice to know how much you have left and to view where the costs are accumulating. To see your current usage, click the Subscriptions tile in the Dashboard of the Azure portal (Figure 1-17).

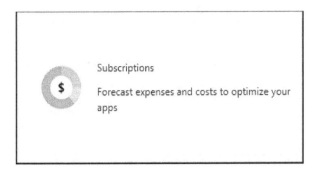

Figure 1-17 The Subscriptions tile on the Dashboard of the Azure portal.

Click this tile to go to the Subscriptions blade, then select the subscription you want to examine. The Subscriptions blade is displayed. On the bottom of that blade is a tile showing the amount left before you hit the cap, what the starting credit was, and the burn rate (Figure 1-18).

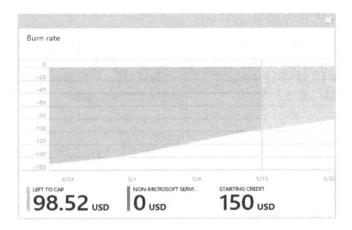

Figure 1-18 The overall cost information for the selected subscription.

We can see that for the account displayed above, the cap is $150 (starting credit), and $98.52 of that has been used so far. Underneath this graphic is the cost by resource. This account is taken up by the

small web app that is running, but if there are VMs, storage accounts, and so on, the total cost of each resource would be displayed here (Figure 1-19).

Cost by resource
AZURE FREE TRIAL

STANDARD SMALL APP SERVICE HOURS - AZURI

**51.48** USD

**100**%
51.5/51.5

Figure 1-19 The cost by resource for the selected subscription.

If you click the graphic, it will show the resource costs by resource in a new blade (Figure 1-20).

Resource costs
Azure Free Trial

↓
Invoice

| NAME | RESOURCE GUID | CONSUMED U... ^ | BILLABLE UNITS ^ | COST (USD) ^ |
|---|---|---|---|---|
| Standard Small App Service Hours - Azure... | 505db374-df8a-44df-9d8c-13c14b61d... | 858.002 | 858.002 | 51.48 |
| Data Transfer In (GB) - Zone 1 | 32c3ebec-1646-49e3-8127-2cafbd3a0... | 0.034 | 0.034 | 0 |
| Data Transfer Out (GB) - Zone 1 | 9995d93a-7d35-4d3f-9c69-7a7fea447... | 0.036 | 0.036 | 0 |
| Storage Transactions (in 10,000s) - Data M... | 964c283a-83a3-4dd4-8baf-59511998f... | 0.456 | 0.456 | 0 |
| Free App Service - Azure App Service | c0f5cb45-6fb1-41c9-8545-72ad400d9... | 2.129 | 2.129 | 0 |
| Standard Medium App Service Hours - Az... | 64d48263-32ab-4359-b05b-8626b097... | 0.013 | 0.013 | 0 |
| Standard IO - Table/ Queue (GB) - Locally... | bd69546d-19b0-4776-865f-8753b800... | 0.001 | 0.001 | 0 |
| Standard IO - Block Blob (GB) - Locally Re... | c1635534-1c1d-4fc4-b090-88fc2672ef87 | 0.001 | 0.001 | 0 |
| Basic Small App Service Hours - Azure Ap... | ba302f7a-078b-4141-a636-a76315ba4... | 0.034 | 0.034 | 0 |

Figure 1-20 The details of the cost by resource for the selected subscription.

The ability to view the billing information on a regular basis is helpful when managing the costs for your Azure subscription. If you have a subscription with a monthly credit, you can tell when you're getting close to the cap. You can also tell where your costs are accumulating. Also, if you provision some VMs and forget they're out there, you'll be able to see them because they will have billing associated with them.

## AZURE BILLING APIS

In addition to viewing the billing in the portal, you can access the billing information programmatically through the Azure Billing REST APIs for a specific subscription. There are two APIs that you can use.

- The Azure Usage API enables you to retrieve your usage data. You can fine-tune the billing usage information retrieved to be grouped by resource if you have used the resource tags that can be set through most of the Settings screens. For example, you can tag each of the resources in a resource group with a department name or project name, then track the costs specifically for that one tag.

- The Azure RateCard API enables you to list all of the resources that you can use, along with the metadata and pricing information about each of those resources.

To get you started, there are Billing API code samples on GitHub that you can download and try out. They are located here: https://github.com/Azure/BillingCodeSamples.

## AZURE DOCUMENTATION AND SAMPLES

In this section, we'll talk about the Azure documentation and samples, including where you can find them and how you can contribute bug fixes, changes, or even entirely new articles and samples to the Azure community.

## DOCUMENTATION

The Azure documentation can be found at http://azure.microsoft.com. This is the conceptual documentation, which explains the services, how they work, how to use them, and so on. The reference documentation is on MSDN (http://msdn.microsoft.com). For example, the documentation for the REST APIs is on MSDN, and it shows every command and all of their options.

All of the conceptual documentation at azure.microsoft.com resides on GitHub. You can contribute to the documentation by adding articles or modifying articles to include information you believe will be helpful to others. To view the contributor guide and the current documentation, please go to https://github.com/Azure/azure-content.

## SAMPLES

In addition to the documentation, there are many Azure samples to help you get started with Azure, also stored in GitHub. For example, Azure Storage has getting-started samples for .NET and Java for Blob storage, Table storage, Queue storage, and File storage. You can use these samples to help you, and you can also contribute to this repository. These samples can be found here: http://github.com/azure-samples.

For the Resource Manager resources, there is a repository of quick start templates available here: https://github.com/Azure/azure-quickstart-templates. This has templates for creating many resources such as the Azure Content Delivery Network, Azure Key Vault, virtual machines, virtual networks, and storage accounts.

# CHAPTER 2

# AZURE APP SERVICE AND WEB APPS

In this chapter, we take a look at the Azure App Service, consisting of Web Apps, Logic Apps, Mobile Apps, API Apps, and Function Apps. We focus on Web Apps and how they work together with the App Service. We create a web app and publish it to Azure. We also look at the options for prebuilt web apps offered by Azure.

## APP SERVICE AND APP SERVICE PLANS

Before we talk about Web Apps, let's talk about App Service and the App Service plans.

## WHAT IS AN APP SERVICE?

The App Service is a service that hosts one of five kinds of applications:

- Web Apps
- Mobile Apps
- Logic Apps
- API Apps
- Function Apps

Each app runs in its own app service. When you look in the Azure portal to see your website, you will look for the app service in which it is running. It conveniently has the same name as the app it's hosting.

## SO WHAT IS AN APP SERVICE PLAN?

An App Service plan defines the capacity and resources to be shared among one or more app services that are assigned to that plan.

The following are some of the criteria you can define when creating an App Service plan.

- Location (such as West US)

- Instance count

- Pricing tier (such as Free, Standard, or Premium) providing distinct settings for a variety of performance and service capabilities:

- Number of cores or instance size

- Amount of memory

- Amount of storage

- Maximum number of instances

- Autoscaling options (depends on tier—automatic, manual, or none)

When you deploy your app service for the first time, you specify which App Service plan you want to use. At deployment time, you can select an App Service plan you have created or create a new App Service plan.

## HOW DOES THIS HELP YOU?

With infrastructure as a service (IaaS), you can create your own virtual machines (VMs), deploy your apps to them, and deal with the IIS setup and application pools and so on. Then, every time you change an app, you have to deploy it to all the VMs again. If you scale it out, and you have four VMs or eight VMs, it just becomes more onerous. With IaaS, you are responsible for the continuing management of your service. Using App Service plans enables you to run multiple applications on one set of VMs, even if each of the applications is deployed separately.

For example, let's say you have five websites and three mobile apps that you want to host. You could run each one on its own VM, which would require 8 VMs. If you wanted redundancy (recommended), that would require 16 VMs. Even if you select small instances, the cost adds up really quickly. Plus, you have to scale each set of VMs separately.

If you could run those eight applications on the same set of two VMs, it would be more cost-effective and easier to manage. This is what using App Service plans does for you. You set up one App Service plan with a specific VM size, number of instances, etc. Then, you deploy the eight applications, specifying the same App Service plan for each one. This results in all eight applications running on that same set of two VMs. You can deploy and update each application as needed—you don't have to update them all at the same time.

When you create your App Service plan, the resources you requested are allocated for you. When you deploy an app to that App Service plan, it simply deploys the applications to those allocated resources.

If you decide you want to have four VMs instead of two, you simply go to the Azure portal and modify the App Service plan, changing the number of instances from two to four. It will create two more VMs and deploy your apps to them for you. If you are using small VMs and want to scale up to medium VMs, you can simply modify the Pricing Tier in the App Service plan, and it will scale up.

With web apps running in an app service using an App Service plan, the management is handled for you, and you can easily scale up and out just by changing the settings of the App Service plan.

## HOW TO CREATE AN APP SERVICE PLAN IN THE AZURE PORTAL

Now, I'll show you how to create an App Service plan using the Azure portal. Later, I'll show you how to create a web app and deploy it to an app service using that App Service plan.

1. Log in to the Azure portal.

2. Click New, then click See All, as displayed in Figure 2-1.

Figure 2-1 Go to the Marketplace to search for a resource to add.

3. It opens the search screen for the Marketplace (Figure 2-2). Type app service plan in the search box and press Enter.

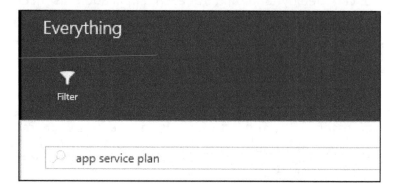

Figure 2-2 The input screen for searching the Marketplace.

4. Select App Service Plan in the search results, as shown in Figure 2-3.

Figure 2-3 The search results for App Service plan.

5. Click Create on the App Service Plan blade displayed in Figure 2-4.

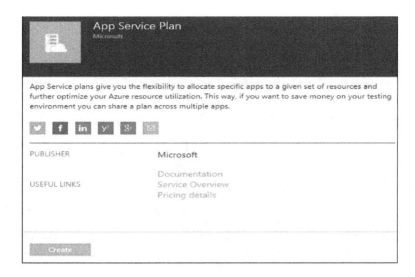

App Service Plan
Microsoft

App Service plans give you the flexibility to allocate specific apps to a given set of resources and further optimize your Azure resource utilization. This way, if you want to save money on your testing environment you can share a plan across multiple apps.

PUBLISHER                    Microsoft

                             Documentation
USEFUL LINKS                 Service Overview
                             Pricing details

Create

Figure 2-4 Click Create to create a new App Service plan.

6. After you see something similar to the App Service Plan blade displayed in Figure 2-5, you can define the parameters for your App Service plan.

App Service plan

* App Service plan
RobinsAppServicePlan

* Subscription
Azure Free Trial

* Resource Group
+ New

New resource group name
RobinBookRG

* Location
West US

* Pricing tier
S1 Standard

☐ Pin to dashboard

Create

Figure 2-5 The fields to be filled in for your new App Service plan.

- App Service Plan This is what you would like to name your App Service plan. Make this something you can recognize when you want to use the plan later.

- Subscription If you have multiple Azure subscriptions administered by this account, this will have a drop-down list of subscriptions, and you can select which one to use.

- Resource Group Resource groups provide a logical container for a related set of resources. For example, you could put all of the resources you create for this book in the same resource group. When you're finished, you can delete the resource group, and it will deallocate and remove all of those resources for you. Let's create a new resource group for our App Service plan; later in this chapter, we will create a web app and assign it to our App Service plan. Leave the value as +New and specify the name of your new resource group. It's recommended that you specify something that indicates what the resources are used for.

- Location This is the Azure region where the resource group will be hosted. This includes metadata such as audit logs, where each resource in the group resides. This can be different from the resources themselves; this is important for those who care about where data is hosted—for example, those in countries with data sovereignty laws. Also, Resource Manager operations are sourced through this region, so you typically want it to be the same as most of the resources in the group. For our example, select the region closest to you.

- Pricing Tier Click this field to see your choices. The new blade (displayed in Figure 2-6) shows the recommended pricing plans. This is a subset of all of the available pricing tiers. If you want to see all of the plans, click View All on this blade. The pricing plan lets you specify the amount of storage, scalability, backup choices, and so on.

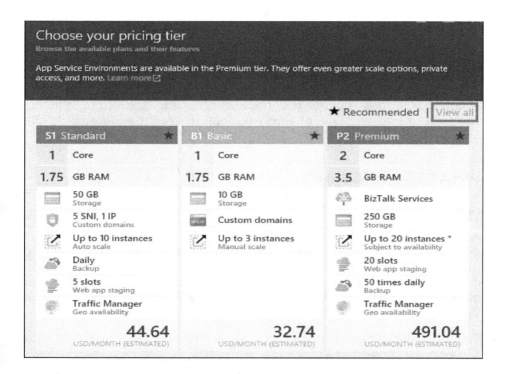

Figure 2-6 The Pricing Tier blade.

Select the S1 Standard pricing plan and then click Select at the bottom of the blade. Now, your App Service Plan blade should display the pricing plan you selected.

7. Select the check box on the bottom of the App Service Plan blade that says Pin To Dashboard.
   This will pin a tile to the Dashboard showing your App Service plan, providing easy access to it. Now, click Create. It creates the plan and adds a tile to your Dashboard.

8. After the App Service plan is created, you can click the tile on the Dashboard and modify it. You can also see what apps are using that plan. After the web app is created and deployed, I'll show you how to scale the apps by scaling the App Service plan.

At this point, you can create one or more app services, such as a web app, and assign them to that App Service plan. They will all run on the same VMs.

# CREATING AND DEPLOYING WEB APPS

Now that you understand App Services and App Service plans, I'll show you what a Web App is, discuss some of its features, and then talk about the various options you have for creating one. Then, I'll show you how to use a couple of those options to create and deploy a Web App.

## WHAT IS A WEB APP?

A Web App is a web application that is hosted in an App Service. The App Service is the managed service in Azure that enables you to deploy a web application and make it available to your customers on the Internet in a very short amount of time. As noted above, you don't directly support the VMs on which your web app runs; they are managed for you. In fact, you don't have access to those underlying VMs.

Supported languages include .NET, Java, PHP, Node.js, and Python. In addition to creating your own web app, there are several web applications available to use as a starting point, such as WordPress, Umbraco, Joomla!, and Drupal.

You can use continuous deployment with Team Foundation Server (TFS), GitHub, TeamCity, Jenkins, or BitBucket so that every time you commit a change, a new version of the web app is deployed.

Scaling is done by scaling the App Service plan to which the web app belongs. You can scale the number of instances in and out on demand. You can configure autoscaling so Azure will scale it in or out for you depending on specific performance measures such as CPU percentage. You can also publish your website to multiple locations and use the Azure Traffic Manager to handle the routing of the traffic to the location nearest to your customer.

For diagnostics, you can gather performance statistics, application logging, web server logging, IIS logs, and IIS Failed Request logs. If you're using Microsoft Visual Studio, you can even remotely debug your application while it is running in the cloud.

In short, there are many features available when using Web Apps to make it easy for you to deploy, manage, and troubleshoot a web application.

# OPTIONS FOR CREATING WEB APPS

There are multiple options for creating a Web App and deploying the content to an app service. Let's look at a few of these, including the following.

- Azure Marketplace This contains all of the resources you can deploy in Azure. I'll show you how you can use this to create Web Apps from preexisting templates such as WordPress.

- Visual Studio Code This is a free, open source, cross-platform code editor with debugging capabilities.

- Visual Studio This is Microsoft's full-featured development IDE.

## MARKETPLACE

There are many pre-created websites and templates in the Azure Marketplace that you can use. To see all of the options available, log into the Azure portal and click New > Web + Mobile > See All. This shows the Marketplace blade filtered for Web and Mobile apps, as displayed in Figure 2-7.

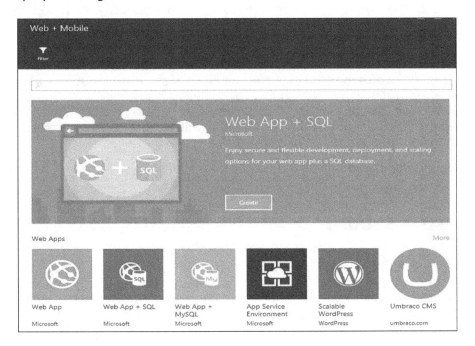

Figure 2-7 Options in the Azure Marketplace for Web and Mobile apps.

If you scroll down on the page, you can see the categories. At the end of any row, clicking More will show additional options in that category. Here are just a few of the choices available:

- Web Apps Web App, Web App + SQL, Web App + MySQL, WordPress, and Umbraco CMS

- Blogs + CMSs Joomla!, Drupal, DNN, Orchard CMS, Umbraco CMS, and MonoX

- Starter Web Apps ASP.NET, HTML5, Node.js, PHP, Apache Tomcat, and some examples like the Bakery web app and the Java Coffee Shop web app

## VISUAL STUDIO CODE

Visual Studio Code (VS Code) is a free, open source code editor with support for development operations such as debugging, task running, and version control. It runs on Windows, OS X, and Linux.

VS Code makes debugging easier, providing IntelliSense code completion and easy code refactoring. It integrates with Git and also package managers, repositories, and various build tools.

VS Code has built-in support for Node.js, JavaScript, and TypeScript. Using extensions, you can use VS Code to debug languages such as C#, C++, Python, Ruby, and PowerShell. There is also tooling for web technologies such as HTML, CSS, JSON, and Markdown.

Using the Azure portal, you can set your web app to get the source code from OneDrive, Dropbox, or a local code repository such as GitHub or Visual Studio Team Service. If you enable continuous deployment for your WebApp, updates will be published automatically when changes are made to your source repository.

You can download Visual Studio Code for Windows, Linux, or Mac here: https://code.visualstudio.com/#alt-downloads.

## VISUAL STUDIO

Visual Studio is a full development environment, giving you the ability to create many different kinds of applications including, but not limited to, ASP.NET MVC applications, .NET client applications, Windows Communication Foundation (WCF) services, Web APIs, and Cloud Services, using languages such as C#, C++, VB, F#, and XAML.

With Visual Studio, you can create a new web application and publish it to an app service in Azure. I'll show you how to do this in an upcoming demo.

## DEMO: CREATE A WEB APP BY USING THE AZURE MARKETPLACE

Let's take a look at how to create a web app from one of the templates available in the Azure Marketplace.

1. Log into the Azure portal. As seen in Figure 2-8, click New on the left side of the page, then click
   See All.

Figure 2-8 Go to the Marketplace Search blade.

2. This brings up the search screen for the Marketplace. All resources that can be deployed to Azure are listed in the Marketplace, including virtual machines, virtual networks, storage accounts, web apps, and so on. As shown in Figure 2-9, type in WordPress and press Enter to perform the search.

Figure 2-9 Search for WordPress.

3. You see a list of matches, as displayed in Figure 2-10.

Figure 2-10 The search results for WordPress.

4. Select the row with WordPress from publisher WordPress. This shows you the blade for
   WordPress; click Create at the bottom to create a WordPress site. You now see a blade where you can start configuring your WordPress site, as displayed in Figure 2-11.

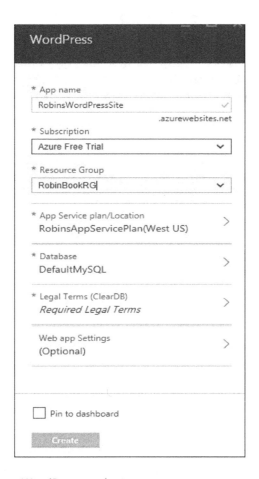

Figure 2-11 Create a WordPress website.

5. Now, start filling in the fields on this blade:

- App Name This is used to create the URL to access your web app.

- Subscription If the account you are using is associated with multiple subscriptions, select the subscription you want to use.

- Resource Group This is a way of grouping multiple resources that are related to one another, such as a web app and a database. Select the resource group you used for the App Service plan you created earlier.

- App Service Plan Select the App Service plan you created earlier in this chapter.

- Click Database to see the database settings, as shown in Figure 2-12. WordPress uses MySQL by default. Set your Database Name and Type (Shared or Dedicated). For Location, select the same region in which your app is going to run. Click Pricing Tier and select the least expensive, which at this time is Mercury. Click OK to save the database settings.

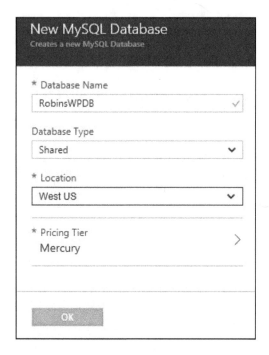

Figure 2-12 Specify database settings.

- Back on the WordPress Settings blade for your new website, click Legal Terms. If you agree with the Legal Terms, click OK at the bottom of that screen, which will set Legal Terms to Accepted.

- You can use Web App Settings (Optional) to set the WordPress-specific settings shown in Figure 2-13; this is optional.

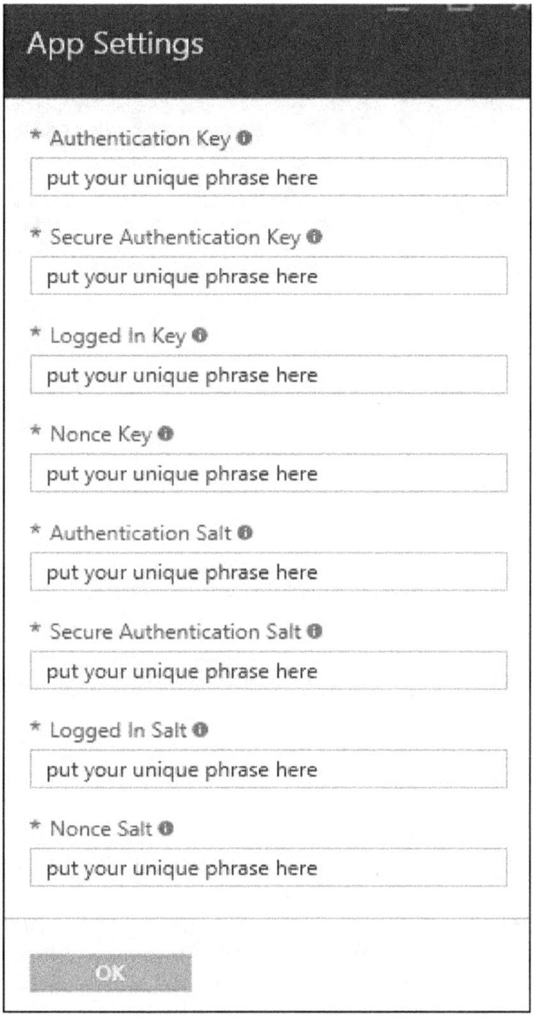

Figure 2-13 Fill in App Settings (optional).

- Back on the WordPress blade, select the check box to pin the web app to your Dashboard, then click Create. Azure will create the WordPress site for you.

6. After Azure has finished publishing the web app, click the tile on your Dashboard to open its properties, as displayed in Figure 2-14. To open the site, click the URL. You are prompted for the rest of the details needed to create your WordPress site, such as language, site title, username, password, and email address. After all the fields are filled in, click the Install WordPress

button. After the WordPress installation is finished, you're ready to go.

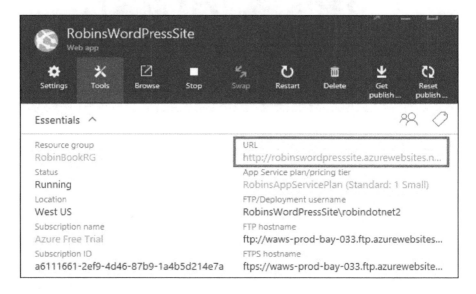

Figure 2-14 Open your new WordPress site by clicking its URL.

Note When your web app is created, Azure also creates an Application Insights instance. Application Insights is an analytics service that monitors your live application. It can help you resolve performance issues and understand how your application is used. Application Insights is outside the scope of this book. You can see the Application Insights instances in the All Resources blade; it will have the same name as your web app, but it will be a different resource type. My list of resources is displayed in Figure 2-15; the ones with the rectangle around them are the Application Insights instances. Note that they have a different icon from the Web Apps. Simply select those Application Insights resources and delete them. (When you select that resource, it will open a bunch of blades. Just close them until you get back to the first one, and select Delete from that blade.)

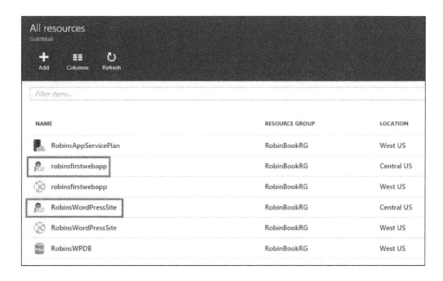

Figure 2 – 15 The Application Insights instances are created automatically when you create a web app.

## DEMO: CREATE AN ASP.NET WEBSITE IN VISUAL STUDIO AND DEPLOY IT AS A WEB APP

To perform this tutorial, you must have Visual Studio 2013 or Visual Studio 2015 installed and the most recent version of the Azure Tools and SDK.

Create a new web application with Visual Studio by following these steps:

1. Open Visual Studio. Select File > New > Project.

2. Select ASP.NET Web Application; the dialog box for creating a project appears, as shown in Figure 2-16. On the right side of the dialog box, clear the Add Application Insights To Project check box. This will prevent the creation of a separate Application Insights instance for this web application.

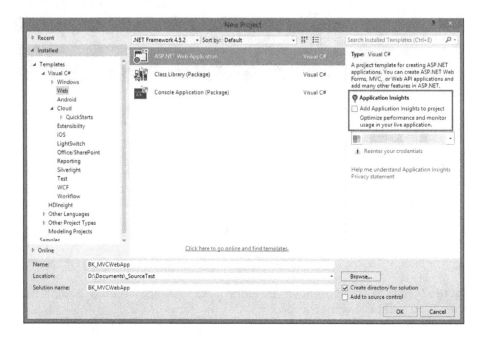

Figure 2-16 Create an ASP.NET Web Application; deselect Application Insights.

3. Specify the Name of the application and the Location for the solution, then click OK.

4. When prompted to select the type of ASP.NET application to create, select MVC from the list of ASP.NET Templates, as shown in Figure 2-17. Clear the Host In The Cloud check box. You will set that up separately. Click OK to continue.

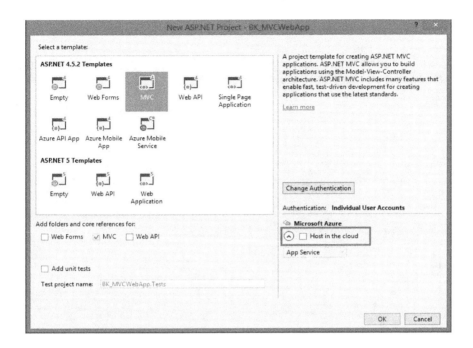

Figure 2-17 Select an MVC application and clear the Host In The Cloud check box.

5. Visual Studio will create a basic ASP.NET MVC application that runs "as is." You can modify it later to make it your own.

6. Now, publish this web application to an App Service in Azure and assign it to the App Service plan created earlier in this chapter. You will create the App Service when you publish the web app the first time. Right-click the website and select Publish (Figure 2-18).

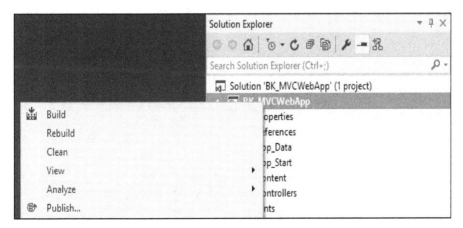

Figure 2-18 Step 1 for publishing the web application.

7. The Publish Web dialog box will be displayed. Select the Microsoft Azure App Service (Figure 219).

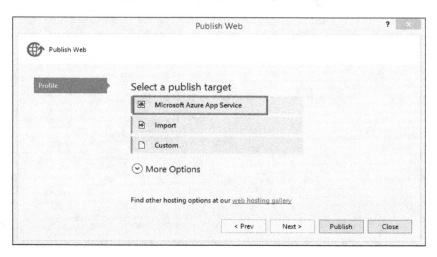

Figure 2-19 Select the Microsoft Azure App Service for the publish target.

8. You will be prompted for your subscription name. You may be prompted again to enter the credentials for your Azure subscription. If the correct account is not displayed, click it to show a drop-down list and add an account if necessary. When the correct account is selected, select the Subscription and be sure the View is set to Resource Group. Open the Resource Group, and you will see the resources that have been set up already. In Figure 2-20, you can see the web apps that I have already created. To publish this application to a new web app, click New.

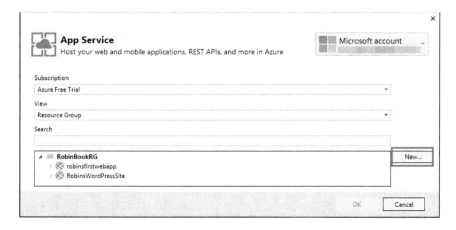

Figure 2-20 Make sure the right account and subscription are selected; show the resources by group.

9. The Create App Service dialog box (Figure 2-21) appears next. Remember that an App Service is simply the host for a Web App, Mobile App, Logic App, API App, or Function App. You'll create a new App Service to host your MVC web application here.

Figure 2-21 Create an App Service to host the MVC application.

- Set the Web App Name. This will be used for the URL for the web app, so select it wisely.

- Select the Subscription.

- Select the Resource Group. If you use the one you created at the beginning of this chapter, then when you're done, you can delete that Resource Group and all of your resources will be removed.

- Last, select the App Service plan that you created earlier in this chapter. This application will be hosted on the same VMs as the other web app(s) you have placed in that plan.

Click Create to create the App Service.

If you look in the Azure portal now, you will see your App Service has been created.

Now let's use Web Deploy to publish our web app to our app service. After creating the app service, the Publish Web dialog box will be displayed (Figure 2-22). You can use the default values.

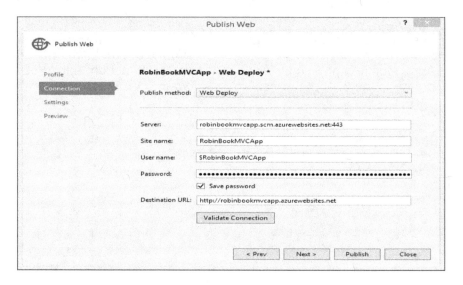

Figure 2-22 Publish settings for the MVC application.

10. Click Validate Connection to make sure the information is correct. After it validates, click Next to go to the next dialog box (Figure 2-23).

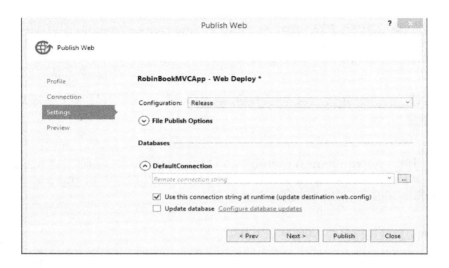

Figure 2-23 Settings used when publishing the MVC application.

11. This dialog box lets you set the Configuration to Debug or Release and provide a connection string to a database if needed. Note that if you are going to use remote debugging on your web app, you will want to select the Debug configuration. Click Next to reach the final page (Figure 2-24).

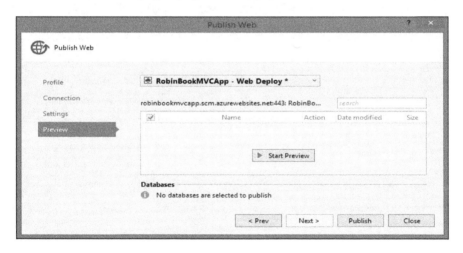

Figure 2-24 Publish the MVC application.

12. You can preview your site here. When you're finished, click Publish to deploy the web application to the App Service. It will open your web application in the default browser after it is published.

When you make changes to your website, you can go through this same process to publish the website again. Note that it will only publish the files that have been added or modified.

## CONFIGURING, SCALING, AND MONITORING WEB APPS

Now that you've created a web app, assigned it to an App Service plan, and deployed it, let's take a look at the configuration in the portal and how to scale your web application.

## CONFIGURING WEB APPS

Log into the Azure portal and go to the web application you created and deployed from Visual Studio earlier. The primary blade should look like Figure 2-25.

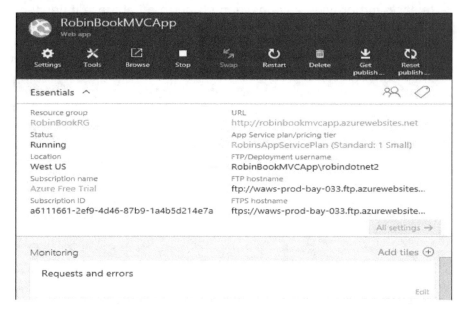

Figure 2-25 Web App blade.

# THE ESSENTIALS SECTION

Let's start with the icons across the top of the Web App blade and look at what they are used for.

- Settings This opens a new blade called Settings. This displays by default when you first open the Web App blade, and is the same blade you see when you click All Settings.

- Tools This opens the Tools blade, which provides access to Performance testing, Process Explorer, Performance monitoring, and so on. It also provides access to the Kudu console, which is helpful for troubleshooting and analysis.

- Browse This opens your web app in your default browser.

- Stop/Start This option starts and stops the web app.

- Swap This option swaps the versions deployed to two different deployment slots. For example, if you have a production slot and a staging slot, you can publish your web app to staging and test it. When you're satisfied with it, you can promote it to production by using the Swap option. When you're sure everything is working okay, you can remove the staging version.

- Restart This restarts your web app.

- Delete This removes the web app.

- Get Publish Profile This retrieves the information needed to publish a web app from Visual Studio.

- Reset Publish Profile This resets the publishing credentials and invalidates the old credentials. These credentials are used for FTP and Git access.

In the Essentials area, it shows the settings provided when creating the web app: the Resource Group, Location, Azure Subscription ID, the URL of the website, and the name of the App Service plan being used. It also shows the credentials for FTP'ing into the web app in case you want to deploy new files via FTP.

Click Settings to open the Settings blade. Let's take a closer look at some of the options on this blade.

## THE SETTINGS BLADE: GENERAL

Figure 2-26 shows the General section of the Settings blade.

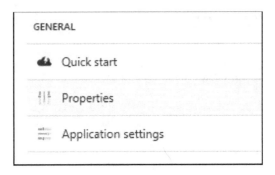

GENERAL

Quick start

Properties

Application settings

Figure 2-26 General section on the web app's Settings blade.

Let's take a look at the General settings we can configure on this blade.

- Quick Start This brings up some resources you can use to learn more about Web Apps. There are links to install Visual Studio and the Microsoft Azure SDK, links to reset your deployment credentials, and links to tutorials, forums, samples, etc.

- Properties This shows some of the same values that are in the Essentials blade: the URL, the mode (Standard), the outbound IP addresses, the FTP settings, and so on.

- Application Settings These are values that apply to your web app.

The top of the Application Settings blade shown in Figure 2-27 lets you set things like the .NET Framework version, PHP version, etc.

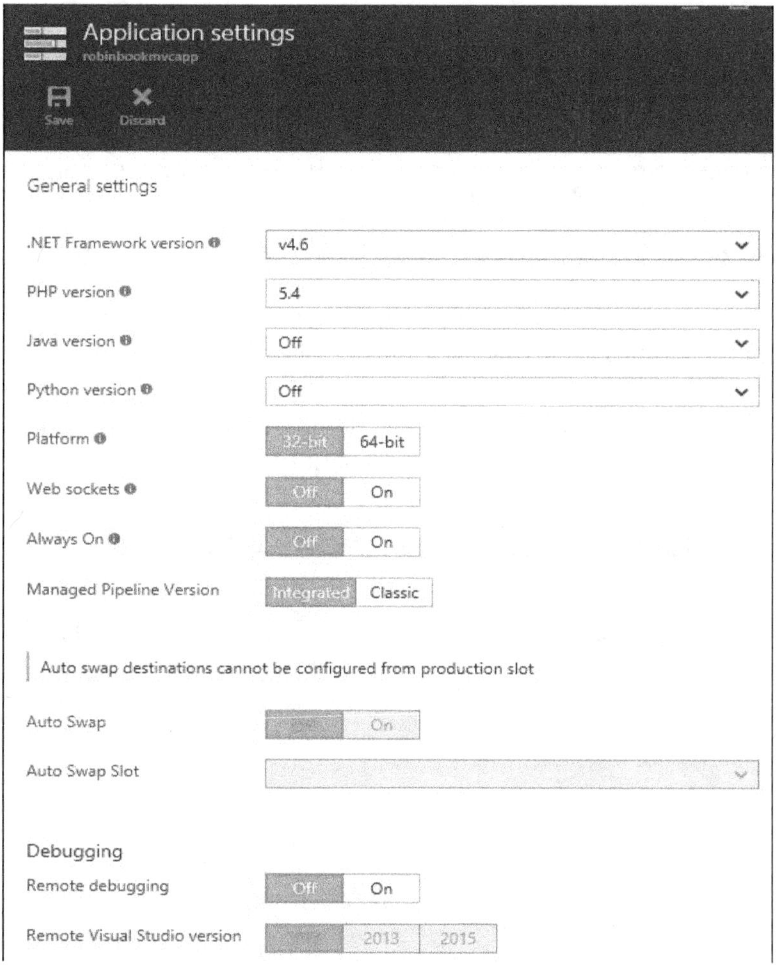

Figure 2-27 Application Settings blade for the web app.

Let's look at what some of these settings are used for:

- .NET Framework Version If your web app is a .NET application, this will denote the major version being used. Values available are 3.5 and 4.6.

- PHP, Java, and Python Versions If using one of these technologies, this allows you to set the version to be run for the App Service. PHP 5.4, 5.5, 5.6, and 7.0 are supported. Java 7 and 8 are supported. For Python, versions 2.7 and 3.4 are supported.

- Platform This indicates whether your web app runs on a 32-bit platform or a 64-bit platform. Note that you cannot select 32-bit for Free websites.

- Always On By default, webpages are unloaded after being idle for a certain amount of time. If you need your webpage to be live and active all of the time, set this to On.

- Debugging These settings allow you enable and disable remote debugging. If set to On, you can then select which version of Visual Studio you want to use to perform the debugging. Be sure to specify the Debug configuration when you publish your web app if you want to perform remote debugging.

Other settings farther down this blade include the list of default documents, handler mappings, and virtual applications and directories.

## THE SETTINGS BLADE: APP SERVICE PLAN

This is the App Service Plan section of the Settings blade (Figure 2-28).

Figure 2-28 App Service Plan section on the web app's Settings blade.

These are the App Service plan settings you can configure on this blade.

- App Service Plan This shows which App Service plan is used by the web app. This will show the settings for that App Service plan, which are the same values you see if you choose your App Service plan from All Resources on the main menu of the Azure portal.

- Scale Up (App Service Plan) This lets you change the pricing tier for the plan. Each pricing tier provides different values for the number of cores, amount of memory, amount of storage, and so on.

- Scale Out (App Service Plan) This is where you can set up autoscaling for your App Service plan and all of its app services. For example, you can ask it to increase the number of VMs if your CPU percentage reaches 90 percent and stays there for X number of minutes. We'll take a closer look at this in the "Scaling Web Apps" section later in this chapter.

- Change App Service Plan This enables you to select a different App Service plan or create a new one.

## THE SETTINGS BLADE: PUBLISHING

Figure 2-29 shows the Publishing section of the Settings blade for a web app.

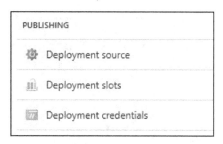

Figure 2-29 Publishing section on the web app's Settings blade.

Here is what each of the Publishing settings is for:

- Deployment Source This is where you can choose a source such as Git, GitHub, OneDrive, Bitbucket, Dropbox, or Visual Studio Team Services to be used for continuous deployment.

- Deployment Slots This lets you publish multiple versions of your web app to different URLs. For example, you can set one up and call it *staging*, then publish interim changes to it. After you've tested the new version thoroughly, you can put the new version in production by swapping the deployment slot called *staging* with production.

- Deployment Credentials This lets you set the user name and password for use with Git and FTP deployment.

There are additional sections for Mobile Apps, WebJobs, and Routing, and a section that enables you to set up a custom domain and SSL bindings.

## MONITORING WEB APPS

Let's take a look at the many ways you can monitor your application. If you're not already there, log into the Azure portal and go to the blade for your web application. Below the properties of the web app is a pane showing the default Monitoring. You can click Edit in that pane to see all of the metrics you can add to that chart and set the time range to be displayed and the type of chart (Figure 2-30).

Figure 2-30 Specify the metrics to display on the chart.

In the Settings blade, you can check out your diagnostics in the Site Metrics Per Instance option. This shows overall metrics for your web app as well as metrics for each instance that is running. You can ask to see the last 24 hours, the last hour, or the last 5 days. This is graphed for you.

You can also see the metrics for all of the apps running in your App Service plan by selecting App Service plan Metrics Per Instance. This has the same settings as the option for your site (24 hours, etc.), but the numbers are combined metrics for all of the apps running.

Another option is Live HTTP Traffic, which will show what's going on currently with the web app, showing Request count, HTTP 5xx responses, and HTTP 4xx responses.

Using the Diagnostics Logs setting, you can enable and disable the different kinds of diagnostics logging for your web app, as shown in Figure 2-31. This includes any logging that the application may do, as well as IIS requests and Failed requests. You can FTP into the site to check the logs; the FTP information is also displayed on that blade.

Figure 2-31 Enable or disable the logging.

# SCALING WEB APPS

Let's go to the Settings blade and look at the scaling options.

> Note You don't scale the web app specifically; you scale the App Service plan, which scales all of the apps running in app services that use that plan.

Scale Up will allow you to select a different pricing tier. This lets you increase the VM size, providing a different amount of memory, storage, etc. that we saw when we originally set up the App Service plan.

Let's take a closer look at scaling out your App Service plan. Figure 2-32 shows the Scale Setting blade that you see when you click Scale Out.

Figure 2-32 Scale Setting blade used for scaling out.

## SCALING OUT MANUALLY

On the blade displayed in Figure 2-32, you can specify the number of instances that you want to run by either editing the text box with the number in it or dragging the slider over to the right. Figure 233 shows an example requesting that the App Service plan should be scaled out to six instances. This means all apps running in app services that are assigned to that plan will now have six instances.

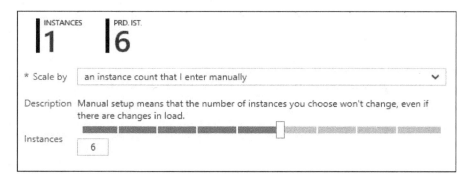

Figure 2-33 Manually scaling out to six instances.

Scaling manually isn't practical unless you're sure your apps will run consistently all of the time. What if you have an application used by a small company, and usage is only high from 8 AM to 5 PM? Do you set it to handle the usage during the day and let it run at that size through the night? It would make more sense to scale down the apps in the evening when there's less usage.

What if you just want to use a simple plan of increasing the instance size when your CPU percentage reaches a specific value, and decrease when the CPU percentage goes back down? You can monitor the app service for these conditions and scale it manually, but wouldn't it be better if you could set it to scale up and down automatically? Figure 2-34 shows the options for Scale By in a drop-down list.

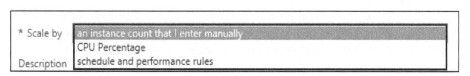

Figure 2-34 Options for scaling out.

You can see that you now have two more options. One is for scaling by CPU Percentage, and other option lets you put in specific rules for scaling.

## SCALING BY CPU PERCENTAGE

Let's take a look at the CPU Percentage scale settings, shown in Figure 2-35.

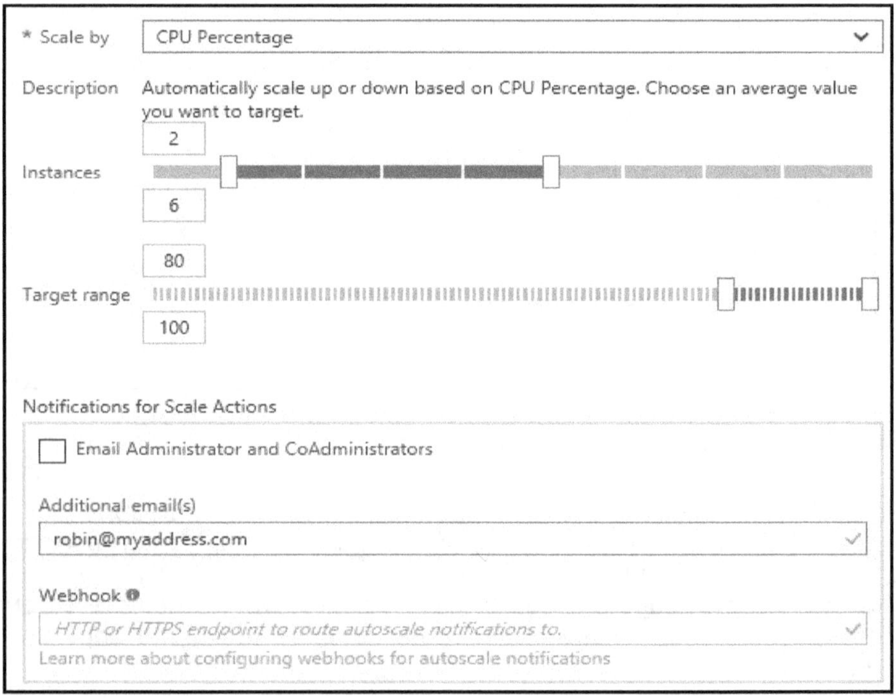

Figure 2-35 Scale by CPU Percentage.

This will allow you to scale up or down depending on the CPU Percentage. You can set the lowest number of instances and the highest number of instances as well as the CPU Percentage value where you want the autoscaling to occur. In the case displayed in Figure 2-35, the web app will run on a minimum of two instances and a maximum of six instances. The autoscaling uses standard Microsoft Insights autoscaling, creating an upper and lower bound rule that you can view using the Resource Explorer in the Microsoft.Insights resource for the App Service. It waits 10 minutes between each scaling action.

In our case here, when the CPU Percentage reaches 80 percent and stays there for at least 10 minutes, it will start scaling up the instances until the CPU Percentage is below the limit or it reaches the maximum number of instances. When the CPU Percentage is below the limit, it will scale down until it reaches the minimum number of instances.

> Note When talking about autoscaling, the average CPU percentage used to scale up or down is the average across all of the VMs running in that App Service plan. This is also true for the other metrics you can use.

You can also set up notifications so it will email you when it starts scaling up and configure a webhook to be run. Webhooks allow you to route the notification to other systems. For example, you could have a service that sends you an SMS message when the scaling begins.

## SCALING BY SCHEDULE AND PERFORMANCE RULES

The third option allows you to set your own rules. You can set a schedule telling when to scale out and in, and you can even combine that with a performance metric. This is very useful when you want to be really specific about how your app scales out and in. For example, let's say that rather than accepting the default amount of time a value is exceeded before a scaling operation starts, you want to set it to a specific value like 20 minutes, or you want to scale using a different performance metric. You can do this by using this third setting, as shown in Figure 2-36.

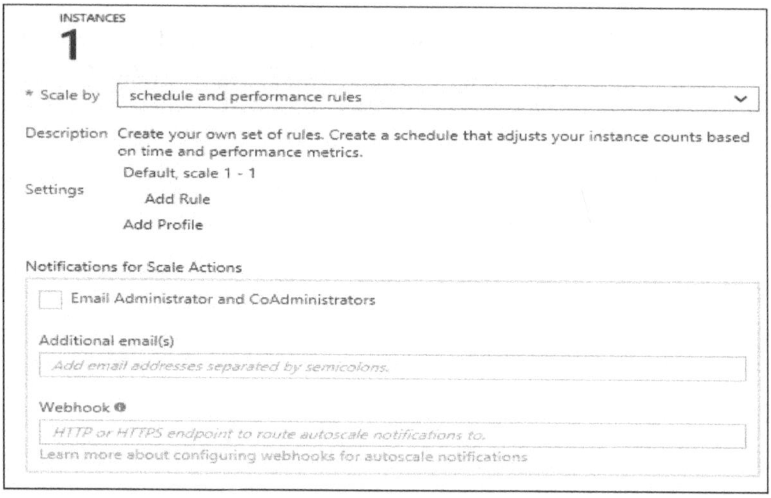

Figure 2-36 Custom scaling rules.

This comes with a default profile called Default, Scale 1-1. Let's edit that profile and then define a rule that will specify that the App Service plan should scale out when the average CPU Percentage is greater than 80 percent for more than 17 minutes, and scale in when it averages less than 50 percent for 12 minutes. (I'm using odd numbers rather than the defaults here so you can pick out the numbers on the screen.) Click Default, Scale 1-1 to change the default profile as displayed in Figure 2-37. After setting up the profile, you'll add the rules.

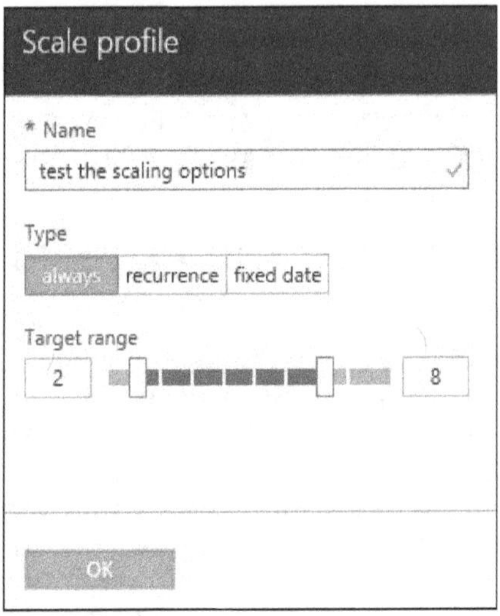

Figure 2-37 Set up a profile for scaling.

This profile is called Test The Scaling Options, and it will apply all of the time. The minimum number of instances is two; the maximum number of instances is eight. Set the fields and click OK to add the profile.

Next, click Add Rule under the profile you just edited. This will bring up a blade similar to Figure 2-38.

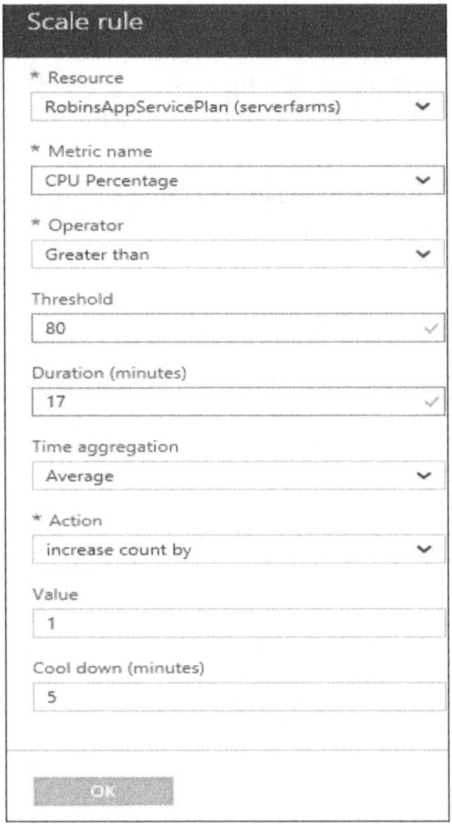

Figure 2-38 Set up a rule for scaling out.

If you click the drop-down list for Metric Name, you'll see several different metrics that you can use to autoscale, such as Memory Percentage, Disk Queue Length, HTTP Queue Length, Data In, and Data Out. For example, if your web application lets people upload data, you might want to autoscale it if they are uploading a ton of data and send a notification to someone who can check and make sure it's legitimate and not a hacker. Set this to autoscale based on CPU Percentage.

In this case, when the average CPU Percentage is over 80 percent for more than 17 minutes, it will scale up by one instance. The Cool Down (Minutes) is the amount of time before another scaling action will take place. So after 5 minutes, if the average CPU Percentage is still over 80 percent, it will add another instance. It will continue to do this until it reaches the maximum number of instances you set on the profile, which was eight. Fill in the fields and click OK to save the rule.

Now we need a rule that says if the average CPU Percentage is less than 50 percent for more than 12 minutes, decrease the instance count. It will keep decreasing the instance count until it reaches the minimum number of instances, which is two in our case. Figure 2-39 shows how to set up this rule.

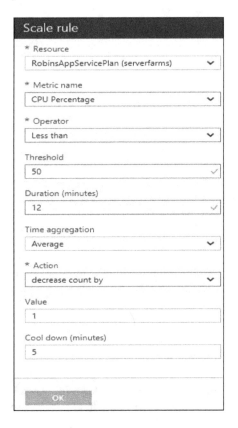

Figure 2-39 Set up a rule for scaling in.

After filling in the fields, click OK to save the rule. Now, the Scale Setting blade should look similar to Figure 2-40.

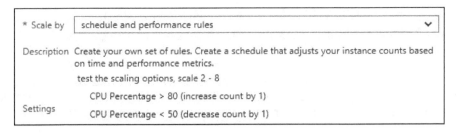

Figure 2-40 A screenshot showing the specified profile and its rules.

Click Save at the top of the Scale Setting blade to save the scaling settings. Now, the App Service plan will scale using these rules. Note that all Web Apps, Mobile Apps, etc. that use that App Service plan will be scaled as the App Service plan scales.

There are two other options for the profile—one is *Recurrence* and the other is *Fixed Date*. Fixed Date allows you to provide a specific date/time range with scaling information. For example, you may want it to scale up faster on opening day for your web application.

Recurrence allows you to specify a start time and which days of the week apply. This is what you would use if you had a web application used by a company from 8 AM to 5 PM but not much after that. You would add a profile to start at 8 AM on Monday through Friday to scale out, and then add one to start at 5 PM on Monday through Friday to scale back in for the evenings and weekends.

If you have multiple profiles, there is an order of precedence in which they are handled. When processed by the Autoscale service, the profiles are always checked in the following order:

1. Fixed Date

2. Recurrence profile

3. Default (Always) profile

In the example above, you would set up a Recurrence profile for Monday through Friday, 8 AM to 5 PM, and then set up a Fixed Date profile for a specific holiday, and the Fixed Date profile will take precedence on that one date.

# CHAPTER 3

# AZURE VIRTUAL MACHINES

Platform as a service (PaaS) is an attractive option for a certain category of workloads. However, not every solution can, or should, fit within the PaaS model. Some workloads require near-total control over the infrastructure: operating system configuration, disk persistence, the ability to install and configure traditional server software, and so on. This is where infrastructure as a service (IaaS) and Azure Virtual Machines come into the picture.

## WHAT IS AZURE VIRTUAL MACHINES?

Azure Virtual Machines is one of the central features of Azure's IaaS capabilities, together with Azure Virtual Networks. Azure Virtual Machines supports the deployment of Windows or Linux virtual machines (VMs) in a Microsoft Azure datacenter. You have total control over the configuration of the VM. You are responsible for all server software installation, configuration, and maintenance and for operating system patches.

> Note The terminology used to describe the Azure Virtual Machines feature and a virtual machine instance can be a little confusing. Therefore, throughout this chapter, *Azure Virtual Machines* will refer to the feature, while *virtual machine* or *VM* will refer to an instance of an actual compute node.

There are two primary differences between Azure's PaaS and IaaS compute features: persistence and control. As discussed in Chapter 2, "Azure App Service and Web Apps," PaaS features such as Cloud Services (that is, web and worker roles) and App Services are managed primarily by the Azure platform, allowing you to focus on creating the application and not managing the server infrastructure. With an Azure Virtual Machines VM, you are responsible for nearly all aspects of the VM.

Azure Virtual Machines supports two types of durable (or persistent) disks: OS disks and data disks. An

OS disk is required, and data disks are optional. The durability for the disks is provided by Azure

Storage. More details on these disks will be provided later in this chapter, but for now understand the

OS disk is where the operating system resides (Windows or Linux), and the data disk is where you can

store other things, such as application data, images, and so on. By contrast, Azure PaaS cloud services use ephemeral disks attached to the physical host—the data on which can be lost in the event of failure of the physical host.

Because of the level of control afforded to the user and the use of durable disks, VMs are ideal for a wide range of server workloads that do not fit into a PaaS model. Server workloads such as database servers (SQL Server, Oracle, MongoDB, and so on), Windows Server Active Directory, Microsoft SharePoint, and many more become possible to run on the Microsoft Azure platform. If desired, users can move such workloads from an on-premises datacenter to one or more Azure regions, a process often called *lift and shift*.

## BILLING

Azure Virtual Machines is priced on a per-hour basis, but it is billed on a per-minute basis. For example, you are only changed for 23 minutes of usage if the VM is deployed for 23 minutes. The cost for a VM includes the charge for the Windows operating system. Linux-based instances are slightly cheaper because there is no operating system license charge. The cost, and the appropriate licensing, for any additional software you install is your responsibility. Some VM images, such as Microsoft SQL Server, you acquire from the Azure Marketplace may include an additional license cost (on top of the base cost of the VM).

There is a direct relationship between the VM's status and billing:

* Running The VM is on and running normally (billable).

* Stopped The VM is stopped but still deployed to a physical host (billable)

* Stopped (Deallocated) The VM is not deployed to a physical host (not billable).

You are charged separately for the durable storage the VM uses. The status of the VM has no relation to the storage charges that will be incurred; even if the VM is stopped/deallocated and you aren't billed for the running VM, you will be charged for the storage used by the disks.

By default, stopping a VM in the Azure portal puts the VM into a Stopped (Deallocated) state. If you want to stop the VM but keep it allocated, you will need to use a PowerShell cmdlet or Azure command-line interface (CLI) command.

## STOPPING AN AZURE VM

To stop a VM but keep it provisioned, you would need to use the Stop-AzureRmVM PowerShell cmdlet such as in the following example:

Stop-AzureRmVM -Name "AzEssentialDev3" -ResourceGroup "AzureEssentials" -StayProvisioned

For classic VMs, a similar cmdlet, Stop-AzureVM, would be used.

When using the Azure CLI, there are two commands used to control the stopped state of a VM: azure vm stop and azure vm deallocate.

Shutting down the VM from the operating system of the VM will also stop the VM but will not deallocate the VM.

> Note The Azure Hybrid Use Benefit program may offer additional savings by allowing you bring your on-premises Windows Server licenses to Azure. For more information, please see https://azure.microsoft.com/pricing/hybrid-use-benefit/.

## SERVICE LEVEL AGREEMENT

As of the time of this writing, Microsoft offers a 99.95 percent connectivity service level agreement (SLA) for multiple-instance VMs deployed in an availability set. That means that for the SLA to apply, there must be at least two instances of the VM deployed within an availability set. Additional details pertaining to availability sets for Azure Virtual Machines are discussed later in this chapter.

> See Also See the SLA at http://azure.microsoft.com/support/legal/sla/ for full details.

## VIRTUAL MACHINE MODELS

As you may recall from earlier in this book, there are two models for working with many Azure resources: Azure Resource Manager (ARM) and Azure Service Management (often referred to as the classic model or ASM). Please see Chapter 1, "Getting started with Microsoft Azure," for a more detailed overview. It is recommended that you use the Resource Manager model for new deployments. The classic model is still supported; however, the newest innovations will be made available only for the Resource Manager model.

For the purposes of this chapter, both models are covered, but the emphasis is on the Resource Manager model.

There are significant and fundamental differences in working with Azure Virtual Machines in these models.

## AZURE RESOURCE MANAGER MODEL

When working with the Resource Manager model, you have explicit and fine-grained control over nearly all aspects of the Azure VM. You will explicitly add components such as a network interface card (NIC), public IP address, data disks, load balancer, and much more.

You may recall that Resource Manager uses various resource providers to enable access to and management of Azure resources. There are three main resource providers used when working with Azure Virtual Machines: Network, Storage, and Compute.

The Network resource provider (Microsoft.Network) handles all aspects of network connectivity such as IP addresses, load balancers, NICs, and so on.

- The Storage resource provider (Microsoft.Storage) handles the storage of the disks for a VM (in the context of Azure Virtual Machines).

- The Compute resource provider (Microsoft.Compute) handles details related to the VM itself, such as naming, operating system details, and configuration (size, number of disks, and so on).

In addition to explicit control over the virtual machine's components, you have the ability to take advantage of other Resource Manager features, such as:

- Deployment and management of related resources as part of a resource group

- Tags to logically organize and identify resources

- Role Based Access Control (RBAC) to apply necessary security and control policies

- Declarative template files

- Deployment policies to enforce specific organizational rules

- Consistent, orchestrated deployment process

This ability affords you a great deal of control in configuring the environment to your exact needs.

## CLASSIC/AZURE SERVICE MANAGEMENT MODEL

In the classic deployment model, VM deployments are always in the context of an Azure cloud service—a container for VMs. The container provides several key features, including a DNS endpoint, network connectivity (including from the public Internet if desired), security, and a unit of management. While you get these things for free— because they're inherited from the cloud service model—you have limited control over them.

Use of the classic model also excludes the use of the additional value adding features available via Azure Resource Manager (tags, template files, and so on).

## VIRTUAL MACHINE COMPONENTS

Like a car, there are many components that make up a virtual machine. Also like a car, there are multiple configuration options available to suit the specific functional needs and desires of the owner.

The sections that follow describe several of the critical components of Azure Virtual Machines. Additionally, more advanced configuration options will be discussed later in the chapter. But first, the base model needs to be established.

## VIRTUAL MACHINE

It is sometimes helpful to think of an Azure VM as a logical construct. A virtual machine can be defined as having a status, a specific configuration (operating system, CPU cores, memory, disks, IP address, and so on), and state. That logical definition can be instantiated by Azure, and the appropriate resources can be allocated to bring that VM to life.

# DISKS

Azure VMs use attached VHDs to provide durable storage. There are two types of VHDs used in Azure Virtual Machines:

* Image A VHD that is a template for the creation of a new Azure VM. As a template, it does not have settings such as a machine name, administrative user, and so on. More information on creating and using images is provided later in this chapter.

* Disk A possibly bootable VHD that can be used as a mountable disk for a VM. There are two types of disks: an OS disk and a data disk.

All durable disks (the OS disk and data disks) are backed by page blobs in Azure Storage. Therefore, the disks inherit the benefits of blob storage: high availability, durability, and geo-redundancy options. Blob storage provides a mechanism by which data can be stored safely for use by the VM. The disks can be mounted as drives on the VM. The Azure platform will hold an infinite lease on the page blob to prevent accidental deletion of the page blob containing the VHD, the related container, or the storage account.

## STANDARD AND PREMIUM STORAGE

The disk files (.vhd files) can be backed by either Standard or Premium Storage accounts in Azure. Azure Premium Storage leverages solid-state disks (SSDs) to enable high performance and low latency for VMs running I/O-intensive workloads. Standard storage is available for all VM sizes, while Premium storage is available for DS, DSv2, F, and GS-series VMs only. Standard storage can also be used with DS, DSv2, F, and GS-series VMs, in which case only the local, ephemeral drive runs on an SSD.

In general, it is recommended to use Azure Premium Storage for production workloads, especially those that are sensitive to performance variations or are I/O intensive. For development or test workloads, which are often not sensitive to performance variations and are not I/O intensive, Azure Standard Storage is generally recommended.

For a thorough review of Azure Premium Storage and implications for Azure VMs, please see Chapter 4, "Azure Storage,"

An OS disk is used precisely as the name suggests: for the operating system. For a Windows VM, the OS disk is the typical C drive; this is where Windows places its data. For a Linux VM, it hosts the

/dev/sda1 partition used for the root directory. The maximum size for an OS disk is currently 1,023 GB.

The other type of disk used in Azure Virtual Machines is a data disk. The data disk is also used precisely as the name would suggest: for storing a wide range of data. The maximum size for a data disk is also 1,023 GB. Multiple data disks can be attached to an Azure VM, although the maximum number varies by VM size—typically two disks per CPU. The data disks are often used for storing application data, such as data belonging to your custom application, or server software, such as Microsoft SQL Server and the related data and log files. Multiple data disks can be made into a disk array using Storage Spaces on Windows or mdadm on Linux.

Azure Virtual Machines also include a temporary disk on the physical host that is not persisted to Azure Storage. The temporary disk is a physical disk located within the chassis of the server. Depending on the type of VM created, the temporary disk may be either a traditional HDD platter or an SSD. The temporary disk should be used only for temporary (or replicated) data because the data will be lost in the event of a failure of the physical host or when the VM is stopped/deallocated. Figure 3-1 shows the various disk types.

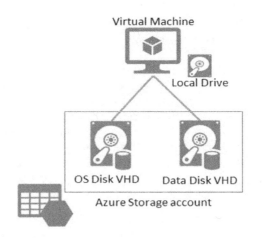

Figure 3-1 Disk types in Azure Virtual Machines.

## VIRTUAL NETWORK

In an on-premises physical infrastructure, you may have many components that all allow you to operate your virtual machines in a scalable and secure manner. These components could include equipment such as separate network spaces for Internet-facing and backend servers, load balancers, firewalls, and more. Many of these components can logically be deployed in an Azure Virtual Network (often referred to as VNET). Azure Virtual Network provides many similar features, such as the following:

- Subnet A subnet is a range of IP addresses within a virtual network. A VM must be placed in a subnet within the VNET. VMs placed in one subnet of a VNET can freely communicate with VMs in another subnet of the same virtual network. However, you can use network security groups (NSGs) and user-defined routes to control such communication.

- IP address An IP address can be either public or private. Public IP addresses allow communication from the Internet to the VM. A public IP address can be allocated dynamically— that is, created only when the associated resource (such as a VM or load balancer) is started and released when said resource is stopped—or statically, in which case the IP address is assigned immediately and persists until deleted. Private IP addresses are non–Internet routable addresses used for communication with VMs and load balancers in the same VNET.

- Load balancer VMs are exposed to the Internet or other VMs in a VNET by using Azure load balancers. There are two types of load balancers:

- External load balancer Used for exposing multiple VMs to the Internet in highly available manner.

- Internal load balancer Used for exposing multiple VMs to other VMs in the same VNET in a highly available manner.

- Network security group A NSG allows you to create rules that control (approve or deny) inbound and outbound network traffic to network interface cards (NICs) of a VM or subnets.

When creating a VM in Azure using the Resource Manager model, it is required that the VM be placed within an Azure Virtual Network (VNET). You will decide to use an existing VNET (or create a new one), the subnet to use, the IP address, if there is a load balancer or not, the number of NICs, and how network security is handled, as depicted in Figure 3-2. While it may seem like a lot just to get a VM deployed, these are important aspects to consider for the accessibility and security of the VM.

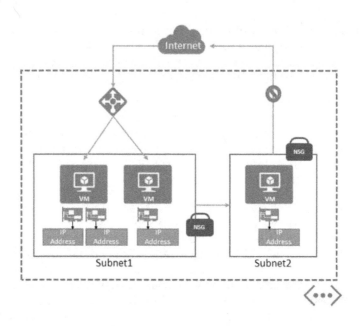

Figure 3-2 VMs in the Resource Manager model have explicit control over related network components.

Classic VMs can also be placed in an Azure Virtual Network. However, this is not a requirement (as it is with VMs in the Resource Manager model).

## IP ADDRESS

In the Resource Manager model, by default, a VM does not have an IP address. One must be explicitly granted to a VM via an associated NIC. A VM requires an IP address to support communication with other VMs in the virtual network or the public Internet.

Each NIC has an associated private address (often referred to as a DIP, or dynamic IP) used to connect to the virtual network and is optionally associated with a public IP address connected directly to the public Internet. By default, these dynamic IP addresses are lost when the VM is stopped/deallocated, but both may be declared as static to make them persist unchanged throughout the shutdown/deallocation of the VM. This is useful for VMs that need permanent DIPs, such as Microsoft SQL Server, DNS server VMs, or permanent public IP addresses. Multiple NICs, each with their own DIPs, can be attached to a VM if more than one DIP is needed—for example, to multi-home a VM in multiple subnets.

In the classic model, the story is similar except that NICs and public IP addresses can only exist in the context of a VM—that is, they are not independent resources. Furthermore, in the classic model, it is more usual to have Internet connectivity provided by the Azure Load Balancer rather than through a public IP Address.

## AZURE LOAD BALANCER

As mentioned previously, the Azure Load Balancer is used to provide a relatively even distribution of network traffic across a set of (often similarly configured or related) VMs. Using the load balancer allows you to have multiple VMs work together—for example, as a collection of web servers in a web farm environment. With a load-balanced set (of VMs), incoming requests are distributed across the available VMs instead of being routed to a single VM.

There are two types of load balancers available in Azure: an external load balancer and an internal load balancer, as depicted in Figure 3-3. The external load balancer is used for distributing traffic from the Internet across one or more VMs. This enables you to expose your application in a highly scalable and highly available manner.

The internal load balancer is used to distribute traffic from within a virtual network across a set of VMs. For example, this could be traffic to a web API or database cluster that should be available only to front-end web servers, not to the public Internet.

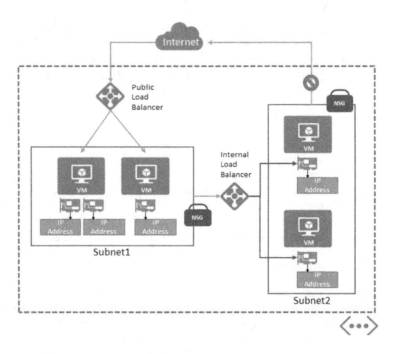

Figure 3-3 Use of both an external and an internal load balancer.

In the Resource Manager model, to use a load balancer, several additional items must first be created:

- Public IP address for the incoming network traffic (for an external load balancer)

- A pool of backend (private) IP addresses associated to NICs for the VMs

- Rules to define the mapping of a public port on the load balancer to a port in the backend pool

- Inbound NAT rules to define the mapping of a public port on the load balancer to a specific VM in the pool

- Health probes to determine if a VM in the pool is healthy

In the classic model, the external load balancer is provided automatically as part of the cloud service model. All VMs in the cloud service are automatically configured to use the load balancer if they expose a public endpoint. Classic VMs can also use an internal load balancer.

# NETWORK INTERFACE CARD (NIC)

A network interface card (NIC) provides network access to resources in an Azure virtual network. A NIC is a standalone resource, but it must be associated with a VM to provide network access (a NIC by itself is of little value). The maximum number of NICs attached to a VM is dependent on the size of the selected VM.

There are several important points to be aware of when working with NICs and VMs:

*   The IP address for each NIC on a VM must be located in a subnet of the VNET to which the VM belongs.

*   If multiple NICs are assigned to a VM, only the primary NIC can be assigned the public IP address. Each NIC will get assigned a private IP address (assuming the NIC is not the primary NIC and has a public IP address). The NICs can be in different subnets of the VNET.

*   Any NIC on a VM can be associated with a network security group (NSG).

When working with classic VMs, it is not necessary to worry about the NIC configuration because that is handled automatically as part of the cloud service model and cannot exist outside the context of a VM.

## NETWORK SECURITY GROUPS

Network security groups (NSGs) allow you to have fine-grained and explicit control over how network traffic flows into or out of Azure VMs and subnets.

NSGs allow you to shape the network traffic flow in and out of your environment. You create rules based on the source IP address and port and the destination IP address and port. The NSG rules can be applied to a VM and/or a subnet. For a VM, the NSG is associated with the NIC attached to the VM.

## AVAILABILITY SET

Azure VMs reside on physical servers hosted within Microsoft's Azure datacenters. As with most physical devices, there is a chance that there could be a failure. If the physical server fails, the Azure VMs hosted on that server will also fail. Should a failure occur, the Azure platform will migrate the VM to a healthy host server on which to reconstitute the VM. This service-healing process could take several minutes. During that time, the application(s) hosted on that VM will not be available.

Besides hardware failures, the VMs could be affected by periodic updates initiated by the Azure platform itself. Microsoft will periodically upgrade the host operating system on which the guest VMs are running (you're still responsible for the operating system patching of the guest VM that you create). During these updates, the VM will be rebooted and thus temporarily unavailable.

To avoid a single point of failure, it is recommended to deploy at least two instances of the VM. In fact, Azure provides an SLA only when two or more VMs are deployed into an availability set. This is a logical feature used to ensure that a group of related VMs are deployed so that they are not all subject to a single point of failure and not all upgraded at the same time during a host operating system upgrade in the datacenter. The first two VMs deployed in an availability set are allocated to two different fault domains, ensuring that a single point of failure will not affect them both simultaneously. Similarly, the first five VMs deployed in an availability set are allocated to five different update domains, minimizing the impact when the Azure platform induces host operating system updates one update domain at a time. VMs placed in an availability set should perform an identical set of functionalities.

The number of fault domains and update domains is different depending on the deployment model— Resource Manager or classic. In the Resource Manager model, you can have up to 3 fault domains and 20 upgrade domains. With the classic model, you can have 2 fault domains and 5 upgrade domains.

## CREATE VIRTUAL MACHINES

There are two tiers for Azure Virtual Machines, Basic and Standard. VMs in the Basic tier are well suited for workloads that do not require load balancing or the ability to autoscale. VMs in the Standard tier support all Azure Virtual Machines configurations and features. This tier is recommended for most production scenarios.

The Basic tier contains only a subset of the A-series VM sizes, A0–A4. The Standard tier supports all available VM sizes and series: A-Series, D-Series, Dv2-Series, F-Series, and G-Series. There are also variants of the D, Dv2, F, and G-Series sizes, called DS, DSv2, F, and GS, which support Azure Premium Storage.

Note With the introduction of the F-Series VM sizes, Microsoft announced a new naming standard for VM sizes. Starting with the F-Series and applying to any future VM sizes, a numeric value after the family name will match the number of CPU cores. Additional capabilities, such as premium storage, will be designated by a letter following the CPU core count. For example, Standard_F8s will indicate an F-Series VM supporting premium storage with eight CPU cores (the "s" indicates premium storage support). This new naming standard will not be applied to previously introduced VM sizes.

- A-Series The "traditional" sizes that have been around since Azure Virtual Machines was introduced. These are your general-purpose VMs.

- D-Series Introduced in September 2014, they feature processors that are 60 percent faster than the A-Series, a higher memory-to-core ratio, and an SSD for the temporary physical disk.

- Dv2-Series Introduced in October 2015, the Dv2-Series are the next generation of the D-Series instances. They carry the same memory and disk configuration as the D-Series, yet they are on average 35 percent faster than the D-Series (thanks to the 2.4 GHz Intel® Xeon® E5-2673 v3 [Haswell] processor).

- G-Series Introduced in January 2015, the G-Series VMs are intended for your most demanding workloads. The G-Series VMs feature two times more memory and four times more storage than D-Series VMs and also include the latest Intel® Xeon® E5 v3 processors. G-Series VMs also use a SSD for the temporary physical disk.

- F-Series Introduced in June 2016, the F-Series VMs provide the same CPU performance (the same 2.4 GHz Intel® Xeon® E5-2673 v3 [Haswell] processor) as the Dv2-Series VMs but at a lower per-hour price. The difference with the F-Series is they feature 2 GB of memory per CPU core and less local SSD space. The F-Series can be an excellent choice for workloads that might not benefit from additional memory or local SSD space.

- N-Series Announced in September 2015, the N-Series VMs feature GPU capabilities, powered by NVIDIA. At the time of this writing, N-Series VMs are limited to a private preview.

One of the easiest ways to get started creating Azure VMs is to use the Azure portal.

# CREATE A VIRTUAL MACHINE WITH THE AZURE PORTAL

If you haven't already done so, log into the Azure portal at http://portal.azure.com. At this point, you will need an Azure subscription. If you don't have one, you can sign up for a free trial at http://azure.microsoft.com.

To get started, click New in the navigation section of the site and then the Virtual Machines option in the Marketplace. As can be seen in Figure 3-4, doing so opens the Virtual Machines Marketplace blade, where you can select from a wide range of VM configurations and preconfigured images from Microsoft, Microsoft partners, and ISVs. The images in the Marketplace include official images from Microsoft for Windows-based deployments such as Window Server 2012, Microsoft SharePoint server farms, and more, and select partners such as Red Hat, Canonical, DataStax, Oracle, and many more.

Figure 3-4 The Virtual Machines Marketplace.

For the purposes of this example, select the Windows Server 2012 R2 Datacenter image. If it isn't immediately listed, you can search for the desired image. On the resulting blade, you can read information about the image, including any operating system updates. You will also have the option to choose a deployment model, either Resource Manager or Classic. For the purposes of this example, choose Resource Manager. Click the Create button to proceed with creating your new VM.

Note As Microsoft and its partners transition to the Resource Manager model, an increasing number of images in the Marketplace are only available via the Resource Manager model.

Next, the Create Virtual Machine blade should open and then extend the first blade to configure basic settings. As you can see in Figure 3-5, on this blade you provide several important details about your new VM:

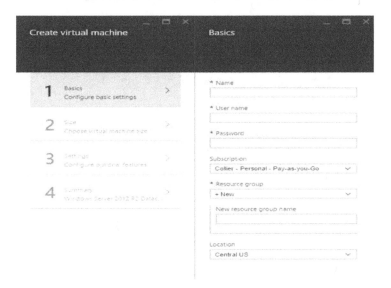

Figure 3-5 Ceate Virtual Machine blade.

- Name The name of the VM

- User Name The administrative user name

- Password The password for the administrative user

- Subscription The Azure subscription to use if you have more than one

- Resource Group Provides a logical container for Azure resources (to help manage resources that are often deployed together)

- Location The Azure region where the VM should be placed

When finished with the Basics blade, click the OK button to proceed to the next step to select your VM size. Not all VM sizes are available in all Azure regions. If a size is not available in the selected region, that size option will show as disabled when viewing all the VM sizes.

After selecting the VM size, you'll move to the third configuration blade, as seen in Figure 3-6, to set up features related to storage, networking, monitoring, and availability.

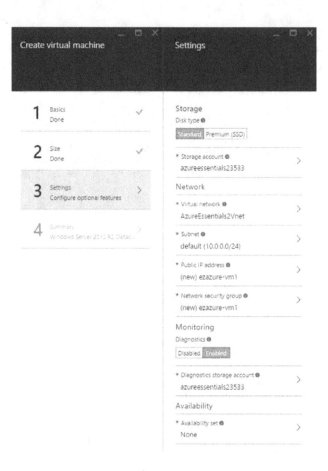

Figure 3-6 Optional configuration settings for a new Azure VM.

Let's walk through several of the important settings in this third blade:

- Storage Select the storage medium for the OS disk in the new Azure VM.

- Disk Type Select either a Standard (backed by a traditional magnetic HDD) or Premium (backed by SSD) disk.

- Storage Account Select the Azure Storage account in which to place the OS disk. This can be a new storage account or an existing storage account.

- Network All VMs in the Resource Manager model must be placed within a VNET.

96

- Virtual Network Either select an existing VNET or create a new one. VMs in the same VNET can access one another by default.

- Subnet Select the subnet (range of IP address from the VNET) in which to place the VM.

- Public IP Address Optionally, chose to create a new public (either dynamic or static) IP address, or select None to not have a publicly accessible IP address for the VM.

- Network Security Group Configure a set of inbound and outbound firewall rules that control traffic to and from the VM. Note that the default is set to allow Remote Desktop Protocol (RDP) for Windows and SSH for Linux.

- Monitoring

- Diagnostics Choose to enable or disable diagnostic metrics for the VM. This setting enables the Azure Diagnostics extension that by default persists metric data to an Azure Storage account.

- Diagnostics Storage Account Select either an existing Azure Storage account or create a new one to which diagnostic metrics are written.

- Availability

- Availability Set Optionally, select the availability set in which to place the VM. This configuration cannot be changed once the VM is created.

Note Diagnostic data (that is, ETW events, performance counters, Windows and application logs, and so on) can optionally be sent to Azure Event Hubs. It is still necessary to enable the Azure Diagnostics extension – new configuration settings are used to optionally send the data to Azure Event Hubs.

The fourth, and final, step is a review step. Once some basic platform validation is complete, you will see a summary of the VM to be created. Select the OK button to start the deployment process. It may take several minutes before the VM is fully provisioned and ready for use.

# CREATE A VIRTUAL MACHINE WITH A TEMPLATE

As mentioned in Chapter 1, one of the key features in the Resource Manager model is the ability to deploy full solutions, using many Azure services (or resources), in a consistent and easily repeatable manner by using templates. Azure Resource Manager templates (ARM templates) are JSON-structured files that explicitly state each Azure resource to use, related configuration properties, and any necessary dependencies. ARM templates are a great way to deploy solutions in Azure, especially solutions that include multiple resources.

As a simple example, if you want to create a solution that requires two VMs using a public load balancer, you can do that in the Azure portal. In doing so, you will need to create a storage account (or use an existing one), a virtual network, public IP addresses, an availability set, and a NIC for each VM. If you have to do this in a repeatable or automated manner, using the Azure portal may not be an optimal approach (due to risk of introducing human error into the process, speed of moving through a user interface, and so on). An alternative deployment mechanism would be to use an ARM template. The example below demonstrates using both PowerShell and Azure CLI commands to deploy the same template.

Deploying an ARM template via PowerShell

```
$resourceGroupName = "azureEssentials2016-VM"
$location ="centralus"

$templateFilePath = "C:\Projects\azure-quickstart-templates\201-2-
vms-loadbalancerlbrules\azuredeploy.json"

$templateParameterFilePath = "C:\Projects\azure-quickstart-
templates\201-2-vms-
loadbalancerlbrules\azuredeploy.parameters.json"
New-azureRmResourceGroup -Name $resourceGroupName `
                -Location $location

New-azureRmResourceGroupDeployment -Name
"My_2_VMs_with_LB" `
                        -ResourceGroupName $resourceGroupName

                        -TemplateFile $templateFilePath `
                        -TemplateParameterFile
$templateParameterFilePath
```

# DEPLOYING AN ARM TEMPLATE VIA THE AZURE CLI

azure resource group create –name AzureEssentials2016-VM2 -- location centralus

azure group deployment create AzureEssentials2016-VM3 --template-file "C:\Projects\azurequickstart-templates\201-2-vms-loadbalancer-lbrules\azuredeploy.json" --parameters-file

"C:\Projects\azure-quickstart-templates\201-2-vms-loadbalancerlbrules\azuredeploy.parameters.json"

The same view of the templates, lacking the integrated search capabilities, is available at https://github.com/Azure/azure-quickstart-templates. The template referenced in the example above can be found at https://github.com/Azure/azurequickstart-templates/tree/master/201-2-vms-loadbalancer-lbrules.

## CONNECTING TO A VIRTUAL MACHINE

After creating a new VM, one of the common next steps is to connect to the VM. Connectivity can be done by remotely accessing (for example, logging in remotely to) the VM for an interactive session or by configuring network access to allow other programs or services to communicate with the VM.

## REMOTELY ACCESS A VIRTUAL MACHINE

When creating a Windows VM using the Azure portal, Remote Desktop is enabled by default. This is enabled via an NSG and the automatic configuration of the appropriate inbound security rule, allowing inbound TCP traffic on port 3389 (the default RDP port). To connect to a Windows VM, select the Connect button from the VM blade, as shown in Figure 3-7.

Figure – 3-4 Connecting to a VM.

This will initiate a download to your local machine of a preconfigured Remote Desktop (.rdp) file. Open the RDP file and connect to the VM. You will need to provide the administrative user name and password set when initially provisioning the VM.

If a Linux VM was created, the process to connect remotely will be a bit different because you will not connect via Remote Desktop. Instead, you will connect via SSH in the standard way for Linux VMs. If you're connecting from Windows, you will likely use an SSH client such as PuTTY.

## NETWORK CONNECTIVITY

By default, Azure VMs are not able to accept requests from the Internet. To do so, a VM must be configured to permit inbound network traffic.

Note Configuring network connectivity sets rules for how network traffic reaches the VM. It does not have any relation to the firewall (software or similar features) running on the VM itself. You might need to configure the server's firewall to allow traffic on the desired port and protocol.

In the Resource Manager model, a VM has inbound connectivity from the Internet if it either has a public IP address on the associated NIC or is the NAT/load-balanced target of an Azure load balancer. NSGs can further restrain that connectivity. To view the NSG rules for a VM using the Azure portal, you will need to start by examining the network interface in the Settings blade for the VM. From there, you would view the Inbound Security Rules on the NSG. There are several blades to move through when viewing this information in the Azure portal. The path would be as follows:

[Your VM] > Settings > Network Interfaces > [Select the NIC] > Settings (for the selected NIC) > Network Security Group > [Select the Network Security Group] > Settings (for the selected NSG) > Inbound Security Rules

In the end, you should get to a screen that looks like that shown in Figure 3-8.

Figure 3-8 The Inbound Security Rules for an NSG on a VM.

Another approach to viewing the NSG configuration is to use the *Get-AzureRmNetworkSecurityGroup* PowerShell cmdlet.

When using a load balancer in conjunction with one or more VMs in an availability set, the connectivity from the public Internet to the VM is controlled by inbound NAT rules and load balancing rules, as seen in Figure 3-9. The rules are part of the load balancer resource configuration, not the VM. The load balancer is configured to work with, or target, the specific VM(s).

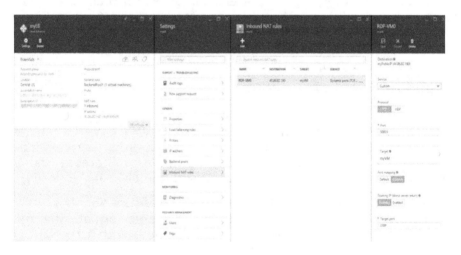

Figure 3-9 The Inbound NAT Rules for a Load Balancer resource targeting a

Resource Manager VM.

For classic Azure VMs, the Azure Load Balancer exposes endpoints for an Azure cloud service. It is the configuration of the Azure Load Balancer that controls how requests from the Internet reach a specific port using a related protocol (such as TCP or UDP) on the VM. This configuration is configuring the Azure Load Balancer to allow traffic from the Internet, creating a mapping between public ports on the Azure Load Balancer and private ports on the VM.

Note NSGs can be applied to both classic VMs and Resource Manager VMs. For the purposes of this scenario on virtual machine connectivity, NSGs are not discussed for classic VMs.

## CONFIGURING AND MANAGING A VIRTUAL MACHINE

Creating an Azure VM is only the beginning. There are several important factors that you should consider to successfully manage the VMs. Factors such as scalability, SLA, disk management, and machine maintenance are all important to consider.

The overall management of the VMs is largely the user's responsibility—you can do pretty much whatever you desire on the VM. Configuration and management of the VM can be done via numerous methods, such as manually via a Remote Desktop connection, remotely using PowerShell or PowerShell DSC (desired state configuration), or VM extensions for popular tools like Chef and Puppet. There is a wide range of choices for configuring the VM—the choice is yours.

## DISKS

As mentioned earlier in this chapter, Azure VMs have two types of disks: an OS disk and a data disk. These disks are durable (or persistent) disks backed by page blobs in Azure Storage. You have several options on for configuring and using the disks for your VM.

Azure Storage uses page blobs to store the VHDs. For VMs that use Standard storage, the VHD is stored in a sparse format. This means that Azure Storage charges apply only for data within the VHD that has actually been written. Because of this, it is recommended that you use a quick format when formatting the disks. A quick format will avoid storing large ranges of zeros with the page blob, thus conserving actual storage space and saving you money. However, if the VM uses Premium storage, you are charged for the full disk size. Meaning, if you attach a P20 disk (which has a size of 512 GB) to a VM and allocate 300 GB for the drive, you are charged the full price for the P20 disk (not just the space used or allocated). Therefore, it is usually wise to allocate the full size for the drive because you're charged for it anyway

## DISK CACHING

Azure Virtual Machines has the ability to cache access to OS and data disks. Caching potentially can reduce transactions to Azure Storage and can improve performance for certain workloads. There are three disk cache options: Read/Write, Read Only, and None.

The OS disk has two cache options: Read/Write (default) and Read Only.

The data disk has three cache options: Read/Write, Read Only, and None (default).

You should thoroughly test the disk caching configuration for your workload to ensure it meets your performance objectives.

## ATTACH A DISK

To add a data disk to a VM, you can start with a new, empty disk or upload an existing VHD. Either can be done using the Azure portal (or using Azure PowerShell or the Azure CLI).

y browsing to the Disks options in the Settings menu, as seen in Figure 3-10, you can view all the OS and data disks that are attached to the current VM. This view also allows you to see the disk type (Standard or Premium), size, estimated performance, and cache setting.

Figure 3-10 Number and size of disks.

To create and attach a new disk, first click the Disks options in the Settings menu to open the Disks blade. On this blade, you will be able to attach a new disk or attach an existing disk.

To attach a new disk, click Attach New. From the resulting Attach New Disk blade, as seen in Figure 311, you will be able to provide several key settings:

- Name Provide your own or accept the default.

- Type A disk backed by either Azure Standard Storage or Azure Premium Storage.

- Size The size of the new data disk (VHD).

- Location The Azure Storage account and blob container that will store your new data disk. You can either select an existing storage account and container or create a new storage account.

- Host Caching The cache option to use for the data disk.

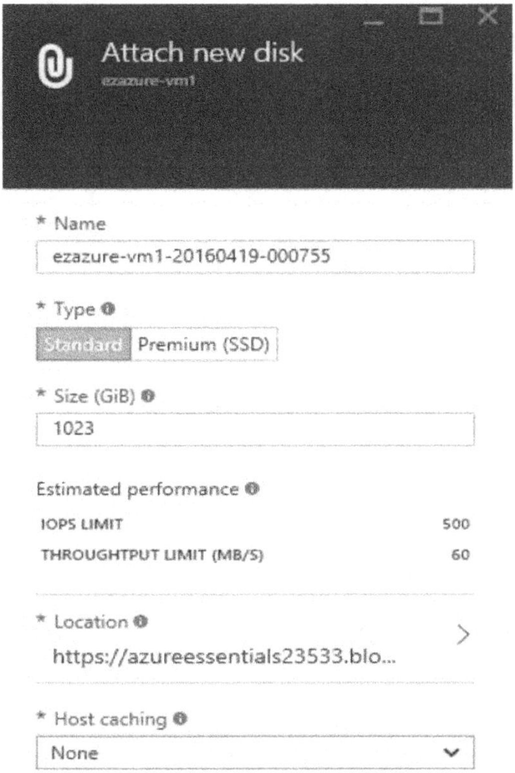

Figure 3-11 Attach a new data disk.

To attach an existing data disk, click Attach Existing on the Disks blade. The resulting Attach Existing Disk blade will present an option to select an existing VHD from your Azure Storage account, as you can see in Figure 3-12. You can use your favorite Azure Storage management tool to upload an existing VHD to a blob container in the desired storage account (be sure that VHD is set as a page blob and not a block blob).

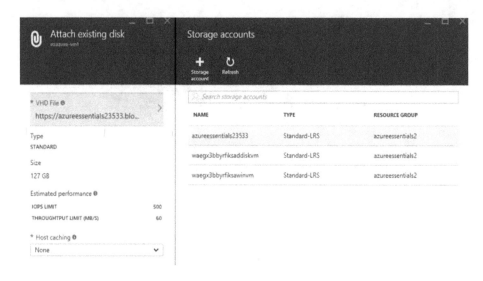

Figure 3-12 The Attach Existing Disk blade.

## FORMATTING DISKS

Once the data disks are attached to the Azure VM, each data disk needs to be formatted (or initialized), just like a disk on a physical server. Because Standard storage disks are billed only for the occupied space, it is recommended that you use a quick format when formatting the disks. A quick format will avoid storing large ranges of zeros with the page blob, thus conserving actual storage space and saving you money.

To format the disk(s), remotely connect to the VM. For a Windows VM, once you are connected and logged into the VM, open Disk Management. Disk Management is a native Windows application that allows you to view the disks and format any unallocated disks. As can be seen in Figure 3-13, proceed by right-clicking the unallocated disk and selecting Initialize Disk.

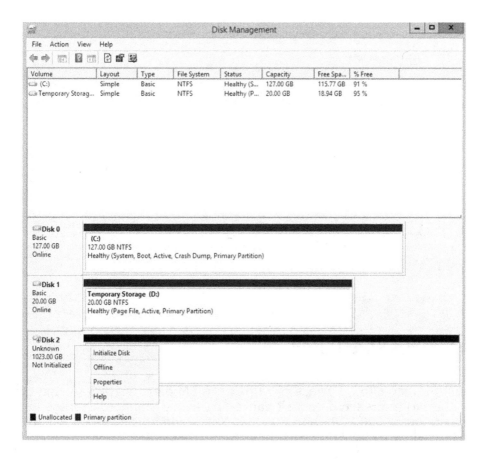

Figure 3-13 Windows Disk Management.

Complete the wizard to initialize the disk. Once the disk has been initialized, you can proceed with formatting the disk.

1. Right-click the disk and select New Simple Volume. The New Simple Volume Wizard should open.

2. Continue through the wizard, selecting the desired volume size and drive letter.

3. When presented with an option to format the volume, be sure to select Perform A Quick Format.

4. Finish the steps in the wizard to start formatting the disk.

## DISK PERFORMANCE

Another factor to be aware of with Azure VM disks is IOPS. At the time of this writing, each data disk backed by Azure Standard Storage has a maximum of 500 IOPS and 60 MB/s (for Standard-tier VMs). For Azure VMs backed by Azure Premium Storage (that is DS, DSv2, F, and GS-series VMs), there is currently a maximum of 5,000 IOPS and 200 MB/s per disk, depending on the specific tier of Azure Premium Storage used. This might or might not be sufficient for the desired workload. You should conduct performance tests to ensure the disk performance is sufficient. If it is not, consider adding disks and creating a disk array via Storage Spaces on Windows or mdadm on Linux. Because Azure Storage keeps three copies of all data, it is only necessary to use RAID 0.

See Also For more information on advanced configuration of Azure VM disks, including striping and Storage Spaces, please review the Microsoft Azure whitepaper available at http://msdn.microsoft.com/library/azure/dn133149.aspx. Although the referenced whitepaper is specific to running SQL Server on an Azure VM, the disk configuration details are common across a multitude of workloads.

# FAULT DOMAINS AND UPDATE DOMAINS

For Resource Manager VMs, you can view the update and fault domains by looking at the Availability Set resource associated with the VMs, as seen in Figure 3-14.

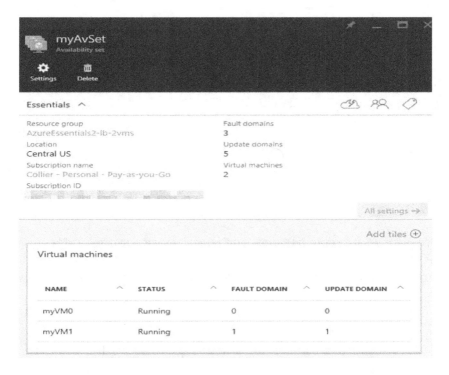

Figure 3-14 Update and fault domains for Resource Manager VMs.

If there is an existing availability set, the VM can be placed within the availability set as part of the VM provisioning process. If there is not an existing availability set, one will need to be created.

Note At the time of this writing, for Resource Manager VMs, the VM must be added to the desired availability set at the time the VM is created. The VM cannot be added to the availability set at a later time.

You can view the update and fault domains used for your classic VMs by looking at the related Cloud Service (Classic) in the Azure portal. As seen in Figure 3-15, the first five VMs are each placed in a different update domain, and the sixth VM is placed in update domain 0.

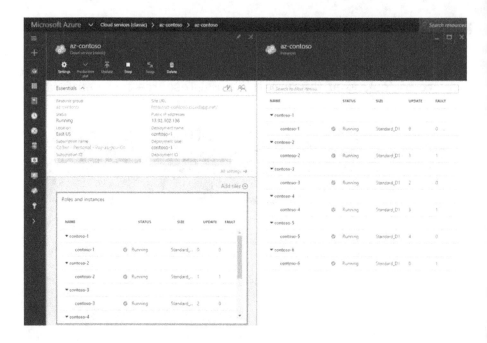

Figure 3-15 VMs, update domains, and fault domains for classic VMs.

A similar view can be found in the Azure classic portal, as shown in Figure 3-16.

## az-contoso

DASHBOARD    MONITOR    SCALE    **INSTANCES**    LINKED RESOURCES    CERTIFICATES

| NAME | STATUS ↓ | SIZE | UPDATE DOMAIN | FAULT DOMAIN |
|------|----------|------|---------------|--------------|
| contoso-1 | Running | Standard_D1 | 0 | 0 |
| contoso-2 | Running | Standard_D1 | 1 | 1 |
| contoso-3 | Running | Standard_D1 | 2 | 0 |
| contoso-4 | Running | Standard_D1 | 3 | 1 |
| contoso-5 | Running | Standard_D1 | 4 | 0 |
| contoso-6 | Running | Standard_D1 | 0 | 1 |

Figure 3-16 VMs, update domains, and fault domains for classic VMs in the Azure classic portal.

# IMAGE CAPTURE

Once you have your new Azure VM configured as you would like it, you might want to create a clone of the VM. For example, you might want to create several more VMs using the one you just created as a template. You do this by capturing the VM and creating a generalized VM image. When you create a VM image, you capture not only the OS disk, but also any attached data disks.

When you capture the VM to use it as a template for future VMs, you will no longer be able to use the original VM (the original source) because it is deleted after the capture is completed. For classic VMs, you will find a template image available for use in your Virtual Machine gallery in the Azure classic portal. As of this writing, there is no view available in the Azure portal for viewing images related to Resource Manager VMs. Instead, you will need look for the image in the same storage account as the original VM (most often the image will be stored at a path similar to *https://[storage_account].blob.core.windows.net/system/Microsoft.Co mpute/Images/[container_name]/[t emplate_prefix]-osDisk.xxxxxxxx-xxxx-xxxx-xxxx-xxxxxxxxxxxx.vhd.*

# CAPTURE A WINDOWS VM IN THE RESOURCE MANAGER MODEL

To capture a Windows VM in the Resource Manager model, you will use Azure PowerShell, the Azure CLI, or the Azure Resource Explorer tool. Capturing a VM is not yet possible in the Azure portal. To capture a Windows VM, complete the following steps:

1. Connect to the VM using Remote Desktop (as discussed earlier in this chapter).

2. Open a command prompt window as the administrator.

3. Navigate to the *%windir%/system32/sysprep* directory and then run *Sysprep.exe*.

4. In the System Preparation Tool, perform the following actions:

    a. From the System Cleanup Action list, select Enter System Out-Of-Box Experience (OOBE).

    b. Select the Generalize check box.

    c. In the Shutdown Options drop-down list, select Shutdown.

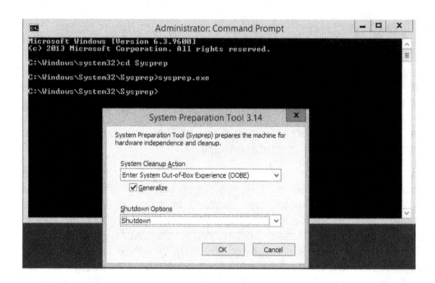

5. The VM will run sysprep. If you are still connected to the VM via RDP, you will be disconnected when it begins to shut down. Watch the VM in the Azure portal until it completely shuts down and shows a status of Stopped.

6. Open PowerShell and log into your Azure account using the *Login-AzureRMAccount* cmdlet.

Optionally, select the necessary Azure subscription using the *Select-AzureRMSubscription* cmdlet.

7. Stop and deallocate the VM's resources by using the *Stop-AzureRmVM* cmdlet, as seen in the example below. The VM's status will change from Stopped to Stopped (Deallocated).

> Stop-AzureRmVM -ResourceGroupName AzureEssentials2-vm -Name ezazure3

8. Set the status of the VM to Generalized by using the *Set-AzureRmVM* cmdlet, as seen in the example below.

> Set-AzureRmVM -ResourceGroupName AzureEssentials2-vm -Name ezazure3 -Generalized

Tip View the VM status using the *Get-AzureRmVm* cmdlet, as shown below. This will show you a *VM generalized* status when the previous command is complete. The *VM generalized* status will not appear in the Azure portal.

(Get-AzureRmVM -ResourceGroupName AzureEssentials2-vm -Name ezazure3 Status).Statuses

9. Capture the VM, placing the image in an Azure Blob storage container folder, by executing the *Save-AzureRmVMImage* cmdlet, as seen in the example below. Note that the value of the *DestinationContainerName* parameter is not a top-level blob container, but a folder under the System container, as can be seen in Figure 3-17. You can also see the full path to the image file by looking in the saved JSON file under the resource\storageProfile\osDisk\image\uri location.

> Save-AzureRmVMImage -ResourceGroupName
> AzureEssentials2-vm -VMName ezazure3 -
> DestinationContainerName myimages -VHDNamePrefix ezvm -
> Path C:\temp\imagetemplate.json

Figure 3-17 The VHD associated with the saved VM image.

Note The saved JSON file is a valid ARM template file that can be used to create a new Azure VM based on the saved image. You will need to add any additional required components, such as an NIC.

With the image safely stored in Azure Storage, you can use this image as the basis for new Azure VMs. To do so, you would use the *Set-AzureRmVMOSDisk* cmdlet, specifying the path to the saved VHD in the *SourceImageUri* parameter. Keep in mind that the image and the OS disk must be in the same storage account. If they are not, you will need to copy the image VHD to the desired storage account. A full example can be seen below (replace with your values as appropriate).

```
Creating a new Azure VM from a captured VM image
$resourceGroupName = "EZazureVM-2016"
$location = "centralus"
$capturedImageStorageaccount = "azureessentials2vm4962"
```

```
$capturedImageUri
=https://azureessentials2vm4962.blob.core.windows.net/system/Mic
rosoft.Compute/Images/myimages/ez vm-osDisk.c55c8313-adf0-
4517-8830-040c402379ab.vhd

$catpuredImageStorageaccountResourceGroup = "azureEssentials2-
vm"
# Create the new resource group.

New-azureRmResourceGroup -Name $resourceGroupName -Location
$location

# !!!! This example assumes the new VM is in a different resource
group and storage account from the captured VM. !!!!

$srcKey = Get-azureRmStorageaccountKey -StorageaccountName
$capturedImageStorageaccount -
ResourceGroupName $catpuredImageStorageaccountResourceGroup
$srcContext = New-azureStorageContext -StorageaccountName
$capturedImageStorageaccount -
StorageaccountKey $srcKey.Key1

# **** Create the Network Resources ****
$publicIp = New-azureRmPublicIpaddress -Name "MyPublicIp01" `
-ResourceGroupName $resourceGroupName `
        -Location $location -allocationMethod Dynamic
$subnetConfiguration = New-azureRmVirtualNetworkSubnetConfig -
Name "MySubnet" `
                -addressPrefix "10.0.0.0/24"
$virtualNetworkConfiguration = New-azureRmVirtualNetwork -Name
"MyVNET" `
                        -ResourceGroupName  $resourceGroupName
        `
                        -Location $location `
                        -addressPrefix "10.0.0.0/16" `
                        -Subnet $subnetConfiguration
$nic = New-azureRmNetworkInterface -Name "MyServerNIC01" `
        -ResourceGroupName $resourceGroupName `
        -Location $location `
        -SubnetId $virtualNetworkConfiguration.Subnets[0].Id `
        -PublicIpaddressId $publicIp.Id


# ****  Create the new azure VM ****

# Get the admin credentials for the new VM
$adminCredential = Get-Credential

# Get the storage account for the captured VM image
```

```
$storageaccount = New-azureRmStorageaccount -
ResourceGroupName $resourceGroupName -Name
"ezazurevm2016" -Location $location -Type Standard_LRS

# Copy the captured image from the source storage account to the
destination storage account
$destImageName =
$capturedImageUri.Substring($capturedImageUri.LastIndexOf('/') +
1)
New-azureStorageContainer -Name "images" -Context
$storageaccount.Context

Start-azureStorageBlobCopy -absoluteUri $capturedImageUri -
DestContainer "images" -DestBlob
$destImageName -DestContext $storageaccount.Context -Context
$srcContext -Verbose -Debug

Get-azureStorageBlobCopyState -Context $storageaccount.Context -
Container "images" -Blob
$destImageName -WaitForComplete

# Build the URI for the image in the new storage account
$imageUri = '{0}images/{1}' -f
$storageaccount.PrimaryEndpoints.Blob.ToString(),
$destImageName

# Set the VM configuration details
$vmConfig = New-azureRmVMConfig -VMName "ezazurevm10" -
VMSize "Standard_D1"
# Set the operating system details
$vm = Set-azureRmVMOperatingSystem -VM $vmConfig -Windows -
ComputerName $vmConfig.Name -
Credential $adminCredential -TimeZone "Eastern Standard Time" -
ProvisionVMagent -EnableautoUpdate

# Set the NIC
$vm = add-azureRmVMNetworkInterface -VM $vm -Id $nic.Id
# Create the OS disk URI
$osDiskUri = '{0}vhds/{1}_{2}.vhd' -f
$storageaccount.PrimaryEndpoints.Blob.ToString(),
$vm.Name.ToLower(), ($vm.Name + "_OSDisk")
# Configure the OS disk to use the previously saved image
$vm = Set-azureRmVMOSDisk -vm $vm -Name $vm.Name -VhdUri
$osDiskUri -CreateOption FromImage -
SourceImageUri $imageUri -Windows

# Create the VM
New-azureRmVM -ResourceGroupName $resourceGroupName -
Location $location -VM $vm
```

For Linux VMs, the capture process is similar. Although you can use PowerShell to capture the VM, a common approach is to use the Azure CLI. You would use three basic Azure CLI commands:

```
azure vm stop -g <resource group name> -n <vm name> azure vm
generalize -g <resource group name> -n <vm name> azure vm
capture <resource group name> <vm name> <vhd prefix> -t
<template file name>
```

As an alternative to using PowerShell or the Azure CLI, you can use the Azure Resource Explorer tool available at https://resources.azure.com. This tool allows you to work against the Azure Resource Manager (ARM) native REST APIs in a user-friendly manner. After signing into your Azure account and setting the tool to Read/Write mode to allow PUT, POST, and DELETE operations (default is Read Only, allowing GET operations), you will need to find the VM you want to capture. Once you've located the VM, go the tab for Actions (POST/DELETE). There, you will find options, as seen in Figure 3-18, to deallocate, generalize, and capture the VM. Capturing the VM will create the VHD for the image and the JSON template file, just as executing the *Save-AzureRmVMImage* cmdlet or *azure vm capture* command would.

Figure 3-18 Capture a VM using the Azure Resource Explorer tool.

# CAPTURE A WINDOWS VM IN THE CLASSIC MODEL

Similarly, in the classic model, there are several steps you will need to follow to capture a VM so it is available for use as a template image. The majority of the steps are the same as in the Resource Manager model. Once the VM has executed the sysprep process (or Linux equivalent), you will be able to initiate the capture process from within the Azure classic portal. Once the capture process is complete, the image will appear in your Virtual Machine gallery, under My Images. You can now use this image to create a new VM instance

## SCALING AZURE VIRTUAL MACHINES

As with most Azure services, Azure Virtual Machines follow a scale out, not scale up, model. This means it is preferable to deploy more instances of the same configuration than to add larger, more powerful machines. The approach for scaling out VMs varies depending on whether you're working with classic VMs or Resource Manager VMs.

## RESOURCE MANAGER VIRTUAL MACHINES

In the Resource Manager model, you don't (typically) scale out VMs in an automated way—at least not how you would with VMs in the classic model. Instead, a different Azure resource construct is used for scaling out VMs: Azure Virtual Machine Scale Sets (often abbreviated as VMSS).

Virtual Machine Scale Sets are a relatively new Azure compute option for deploying and managing a set of identical VMs. You configure all VMs in a scale set in an identical manner. You configure the VM image to be used (operating system configuration, software installed on the VM, and so on) and let Azure provision the desired number of identical VMs (based on the provided image). The VMs in a scale set can run either a Windows or a Linux operating system. Scaling with VMSS does not require the preprovisioning of VMs within an availability set (like autoscale for classic VMs does). At the time of this writing, you can have up to 100 VMs in a VM scale set.

It should be noted that when working with VMSS, there is no data disk available (as you may have with a regular Azure VM). Data should be stored on either the OS disk or an external data store such as Azure Table, File, or Blob storage; Azure SQL Database; Azure DocumentDB, and so on.

VMSS can be provisioned either via the Azure portal or working with VMSS is likely to be the most common approach because doing so offers many more features than are currently available in the Azure portal. For instance, you can configure autoscale rules relatively easily using the ARM template. Such configuration is not yet available within the Azure portal.

Once the VMSS is created, as can be seen in Figure 3-19, you can see that it contains several familiar constructs, such as a load balancer, virtual network, IP address, and multiple Azure Storage accounts.

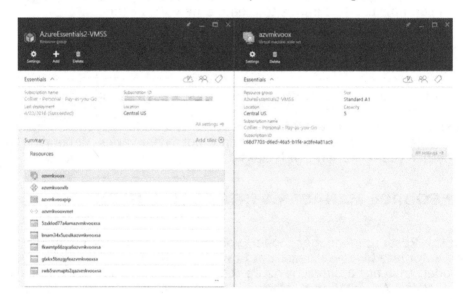

Figure 3-19 A resource group containing assets related to a new VMSS.

VMSS are the preferred way to implement a scale-out compute cluster in Azure. In fact, Azure uses VMSS to host higher-level services such as Azure Batch, Azure Service Fabric, and Azure Container Service.

## CLASSIC VIRTUAL MACHINES

In the classic model, before VMs can be scaled (out or in), the instances must be placed within an availability set. When determining the scale-out approach for VMs, it is important to determine the maximum number of VMs because that maximum number of VMs must be created, configured, and placed into the availability set. When it comes time to scale out, the VMs within the availability set are used to fulfill the scale-out needs. VMs within an availability set should all be the same size to take advantage of Azure's autoscale feature.

# CHAPTER 4

# AZURE STORAGE

Microsoft Azure Storage is a Microsoft-managed service that provides durable, scalable, and redundant storage. Microsoft takes care of maintenance and handles critical problems for you. An Azure subscription can host up to 100 storage accounts, each of which can hold 500 TB. If you have a business case, you can talk to the Azure Storage team and get approval for up to 250 storage accounts in a subscription.

Azure Storage consists of four data services: Blob storage, File storage, Table storage, and Queue storage. Blob storage supports both standard and premium storage, with premium storage using only SSDs for the fastest performance possible. Another new feature added in 2016 is cool storage, allowing you to store large amounts of rarely accessed data for a lower cost.

In this chapter, we look at the four Azure Storage services. We talk about each one, discuss what they are used for, and show how to create storage accounts and manage the data objects. We'll also touch briefly on securing your applications' use of Azure Storage.

## STORAGE ACCOUNTS

This reference table shows the various kinds of storage accounts and what objects are used with each.

| Type of storage account | General-purpose Standard storage account | General-purpose Premium storage account | Blob storage account, hot and cool access tiers |
|---|---|---|---|
| Services supported | Blob, File, Table, Queue Services | Blob service | Blob service |
| Types of blobs supported | Block blobs, page blobs, append blobs | Page blobs | Block blobs and append blobs |

You can view your data objects using one of a number of storage explorers, each of which has different capabilities. While you can view and update some data in the Azure portal, the customer experience is not complete. For example, you cannot upload blobs or add and view messages in a queue. In this chapter, we use the Azure portal, Visual Studio Cloud Explorer, and PowerShell to access the data.

> Note After this chapter was completed, the Microsoft Azure Storage Explorer team released a new version that supports all four types of storage objects—blobs, files, tables, and queues. This is a free multi-platform tool that you can download from here: http://storageexplorer.com/

## GENERAL-PURPOSE STORAGE ACCOUNTS

There are two kinds of general-purpose storage accounts.

## STANDARD STORAGE

The most widely used storage accounts are Standard storage accounts, which can be used for all four types of data—blobs, files, tables, and queues. Standard storage accounts use magnetic media to store data.

# PREMIUM STORAGE

Premium storage provides high-performance storage for page blobs and specifically virtual hard disks (VHDs). Premium storage accounts use SSD to store data. Microsoft recommends using Premium storage for all of your virtual machines (VMs).

## BLOB STORAGE ACCOUNTS

The Blob storage account is a specialized storage account used to store block blobs and append blobs. You can't store page blobs in these account;, therefore, you can't store VHD files. These accounts allow you to set an access tier to Hot or Cool; the tier can be changed at any time.

The hot access tier is used for files that are accessed frequently. For blobs stored in the hot access tier, you pay a higher cost for storing the blobs, but the cost for accessing the blobs is much lower.

The cool access tier is used for files that are accessed infrequently. For blobs stored in the cool access tier, you pay a higher cost for accessing the blobs, but the cost of storage is much lower.

## STORAGE SERVICES

Azure Storage supports four kinds of objects that can be stored—blobs, files (on a file share), tables, and queues. Let's take a closer look at each one of these.

## BLOB STORAGE

The word *blob* is an acronym for binary large object. Blobs are basically files like those that you store on your computer (or tablet, mobile device, etc.). They can be pictures, Microsoft Excel files, HTML files, virtual hard disks (VHDs)—pretty much anything.

The Azure Blob service gives you the ability to store files and access them from anywhere in the world by using URLs, the REST interface, or one of the Azure SDK storage client libraries. Storage client libraries are available for multiple languages, including .NET, Node.js, Java, PHP, Ruby, and Python. To use the Blob service, you have to create a storage account. Once you have a storage account, you can create containers, which are similar to folders, and then put blobs in the containers. You can have an unlimited number of containers in a storage account and an unlimited number of blobs in each container, up to the maximum size of a storage account, which is 500 TB. The Blob service supports only a single-level hierarchy of containers; in other words, containers cannot contain other containers.

Azure Storage supports three kinds of blobs: block blobs, page blobs, and append blobs.

- Block blobs are used to hold ordinary files up to 195 GB in size (4 MB × 50,000 blocks). The primary use case for block blobs is the storage of files that are read from beginning to end, such as media files or image files for websites. They are named *block blobs* because files larger than 64 MB must be uploaded as small blocks, which are then consolidated (or committed) into the final blob.

- Page blobs are used to hold random-access files up to 1 TB in size. Page blobs are used primarily as the backing storage for the VHDs used to provide durable disks for Azure Virtual Machines (Azure VMs), the IaaS feature in Azure Compute. They are named *page blobs* because they provide random read/write access to 512-byte pages.

- Append blobs are made up of blocks like block blobs, but they are optimized for append operations. These are frequently used for logging information from one or more sources into the same blob. For example, you might write all of your trace logging to the same append blob for an application running on multiple VMs. A single append blob can be up to 195 GB.

Blobs are addressable through a URL, which has the following format:

https://[storage                             account
name]/blob.core.windows.net/[container]/[blob name]

The Blob service supports only a single physical level of containers. However, it supports the simulation of a file system with folders within the containers by allowing blob names to contain the '/' character. The client APIs provide support to traverse this simulated file system. For example, if you have a container called *animals* and you want to group the animals within the container, you could add blobs named cats/tuxedo.png, cats/marmalade.png, and so on. The URL would include the entire blob name including the "subfolder," and it would end up looking like this:

https://mystorage.blob.core.windows.net/animals/cats/tuxedo.png

https://mystorage.blob.core.windows.net/animals/cats/marmalade.png

When looking at the list of blobs using a storage explorer tool, you can see either a hierarchical directory tree or a flat listing. The directory tree would show cats as a subfolder under animals and would show the .png files in the subfolder. The flat listing would list the blobs with the original names, cats/tuxedo.png and cats/marmalade.png.

You also can assign a custom domain to the storage account, which changes the root of the URL, so you could have something like this:

http://[storage.companyname.com]/[container]/[blobname]

This eliminates cross-domain issues when accessing files in blob storage from a website because you could use the company domain for both. Blob storage also supports Cross-Origin Resource Sharing (CORS) to help with this type of cross-source usage.

Note     At this time, Microsoft does not support using a custom domain name with HTTPS.

# FILE STORAGE

The Azure Files service enables you to set up highly available network file shares that can be accessed by using the standard Server Message Block (SMB) protocol. This means that multiple VMs can share the same files with both read and write access. The files can also be accessed using the REST interface or the storage client libraries. The Files service removes the need for you to host your own file shares in an Azure VM and go through the tricky configuration required to make it highly available.

One thing that's really special about Azure file shares versus file shares on-premises is that you can access the file from anywhere by using a URL that points to the file (similar to the blob storage URL displayed above). To do this, you have to append a shared access signature (SAS). We'll talk more about shared access signatures in the section on Security.

File shares can be used for many common scenarios:

- Many on-premises applications use file shares; this makes it easier to migrate those applications that share data to Azure. If you mount the file share to the same drive letter that the on-premises application uses, the part of your application that accesses the file share should work without any changes.

- Configuration files can be stored on a file share and accessed by multiple VMs.

- Diagnostic logs, metrics, crash dumps, etc. can be saved to a file share to be processed and analyzed later.

- Tools and utilities used by multiple developers in a group can be stored on a file share to ensure that everyone uses the same version and that they are available to everyone in the group.

To make the share visible to a VM, you just mount it as you would any other file share, and then you can access it through the network URL or the drive letter to which it was assigned. The network URL has the format \\[storage account name].file.core.windows.net\[share name]. After the share is mounted, you can access it using the standard file system APIs to add, change, delete, and read the directories and files.

To create or view a file share or upload or download files to it from outside Azure, you can use the Azure portal, PowerShell, the Azure Command-Line Interface (CLI), the REST APIs, one of the storage client libraries, or AzCopy, a command-line tool provided by Microsoft. There are also several storage explorers you can use, as noted at the beginning of this article.

Here are some of the points about Azure Files that you need to know:

- When using SMB 2.1, the share is available only to VMs within the same region as the storage account. This is because SMB 2.1 does not support encryption.

- When using SMB 3.0, the share can be mounted on VMs in different regions, or even the desktop.
Note that to mount an Azure file share on the desktop, port 445 (SMB) must be open, so you may need to negotiate that with your company. Many ISPs and corporate IT departments block this port. This TechNet wiki shows a list of ISPs reported by Microsoft customers as allowing or disallowing port 445 traffic:

http://social.technet.microsoft.com/wiki/contents/articles/32346.azure -summary-of-isps-thatallow-disallow-access-from-port-445.aspx

- If using a Linux VM, you can only mount shares available within the same region as the storage account. This is because while the Linux SMB client supports SMB 3.0, it does not currently support encryption. The Linux developers responsible for SMB functionality have agreed to implement this, but there is no known time frame.

- If using a Mac, you can't mount Azure File shares because Apple's Mac OS doesn't support encryption on SMB 3.0. Apple has agreed to implement this, but there is no known time frame.

- You can access the data from anywhere by using the REST APIs (rather than SMB).

- The storage emulator does not support Azure Files.

- The file shares can be up to 5 TB.

- Throughput is up to 60 MB/s per share.

- The size limit of the files placed on the share is 1 TB.

- There are up to 1,000 IOPS (of size 8 KB) per share.

- Active Directory–based authentication and access control lists (ACLs) are not currently supported, but it is expected that they will be supported at some time in the future. For now, the Azure Storage account credentials are used to provide authentication for access to the file share. This means anybody with the share mounted will have full read/write access to the share.

- For files that are accessed repeatedly, you can maximize performance by splitting a set of files among multiple shares.

## TABLE STORAGE

Azure Table storage is a scalable NoSQL data store that enables you to store large volumes of semistructured, nonrelational data. It does not allow you to do complex joins, use foreign keys, or execute stored procedures. Each table has a single clustered index that can be used to query the data quickly. You also can access the data by using LINQ queries and Odata with the WCF Data Service .NET libraries. A common use of table storage is for diagnostics logging.

To use table storage, you have to create a storage account. Once you have a storage account, you can create tables and fill them with data.

A table stores entities (rows), each of which contains a set of key/value pairs. Each entity has three system properties: a partition key, a row key, and a timestamp. The partition key and row key combination must be unique; together they make up the primary key for the table. The PartitionKey property is used to shard (partition) the entities across different storage nodes, allowing for load balancing across storage nodes. All entities with the same PartitionKey are stored on the same storage node. The RowKey is used to provide uniqueness within a given partition.

To get the best performance, you should give a lot of thought to the PrimaryKey and RowKey and how you need to retrieve the data. You don't want all of your data to be in the same partition; nor do you want each entity to be in its own partition.

The Azure Table service provides scalability targets for both storage account and partitions. The Timestamp property is maintained by Azure, and it represents the date and time the entity was last modified. Azure Table service uses this to support optimistic concurrency with Etags.

In addition to the system properties, each entity has a collection of key/value pairs called properties. There is no schema, so the key/value pairs of each entity can contain values of different properties. For example, you could be doing logging, and one entity could contain a payload of {customer id, customer name, request date/time, request} and the next could have {customer id, order id, item count, date-time order filled}. You can store up to 252 key/value pairs in each table entity.

The number of tables is unlimited, up to the size limit of a storage account.

Tables can be managed by using the storage client library. The Table service also supports a REST API that implements the Odata protocol; tables are addressable with the Odata protocol using a URL in the following format:

http://[storage account name]/table.core.windows.net/[table name]

## QUEUE STORAGE

The Azure Queue service is used to store and retrieve messages. Queue messages can be up to 64 KB in size, and a queue can contain millions of messages—up to the maximum size of a storage account. Queues generally are used to create a list of messages to be processed asynchronously. The Queue service supports best-effort first in, first out (FIFO) queues.

For example, you might have a background process (such as a worker role or Azure WebJob) that continuously checks for messages on a queue. When it finds a message, it processes the message and then removes it from the queue. One of the most common examples is image or video processing.

Let's say you have a web application that allows a customer to upload images into a container in blob storage. Your application needs to create thumbnails for each image. Rather than making the customer wait while this processing is done, you put a message on a queue with the customer ID and container name. Then, you have a background process that retrieves the message and parses it to get the customer ID and the container name. The background process then retrieves each image, creates a thumbnail, and writes the thumbnail back to the same blob storage container as the original image. After all images are processed, the background process removes the message from the queue.

What if you need the message to exceed 64 KB in size? In that case, you could write a file with the information to a blob in blob storage and put the URL to the file in the queue message. The background process could retrieve the message from the queue and then take the URL and read the file from blob storage to do the required processing.

Azure Queues provide at-least-once semantics in which each message may be read one or more times. This makes it important that all processing of the message be idempotent, which means the outcome of the processing must be the same regardless of how many times the message is processed.

When you retrieve a message from a queue, it is not deleted from the queue—you have to delete it when you're done with it. When the message is read from the queue, it becomes invisible. The Invisibility Timeout is the amount of time to allow for processing the message—if the message is not deleted from the queue within this amount of time, it becomes visible again for processing. In general, you want to set this property to the largest amount of time that would be needed to process a message so that while one instance of a worker role is processing it, another instance doesn't find it (visible) on the queue and try to process it at the same time.

You don't want to read the message from the queue, delete it from the queue, and then start processing it. If the receiver fails, that queue entry will never be processed. Leaving the message on the queue (but invisible) until the processing has completed handles the case of the receiving process failing—eventually, the message will become visible again and will be processed by another instance of the receiver.

You can simulate a workflow by using a different queue for each step. A message can be processed from one queue from which it is deleted on completion, and then that processing can place a new message on a different queue to initiate processing for the next step in the workflow. You can also prioritize messages by using queues and processing the messages in them with different priorities.

The Queue service provides poison message support through the dequeue count. The concern is that an invalid message could cause an application handling it to crash, causing the message to become visible on the queue again only to crash the application again the next time the message is processed. Such a message is referred to as a *poison message*. You can prevent this by checking the dequeue count for the message. If this exceeds some level, the processing of the message should be stopped, the message deleted from the queue, and a copy inserted in a separate poison message queue for offline review. You could process those entries periodically and send an email when an entry is placed on the queue, or you could just let them accumulate and check them manually.

If you want to process the queue messages in batches, you can retrieve up to 32 messages in one call and then process them individually. Note, however, that when you retrieve a batch of messages, it sets the Invisibility Timeout for all of the messages to the same time. This means you must be able to process all of them within the time allotted.

## REDUNDANCY

What happens if the storage node on which your blobs are stored fails? What happens if the rack holding the storage node fails? Fortunately, Azure supports something called *redundancy*. There are four choices for redundancy; you specify which one to use when you create the storage account. You can change the redundancy settings after they are set up, except in the case of zone redundant storage.

- Locally Redundant Storage (LRS) Azure Storage provides high availability by ensuring that three copies of all data are made synchronously before a write is deemed successful. These copies are stored in a single facility in a single region. The replicas reside in separate fault domains and upgrade domains. This means the data is available even if a storage node holding your data fails or is taken offline to be updated.

  When you make a request to update storage, Azure sends the request to all three replicas and waits for successful responses for all of them before responding to you. This means that the copies in the primary region are always in sync.

  LRS is less expensive than GRS, and it also offers higher throughput. If your application stores data that can be easily reconstructed, you may opt for LRS.

- Geo-Redundant Storage (GRS) GRS makes three synchronous copies of the data in the primary region for high availability, and then it asynchronously makes three replicas in a paired region for disaster recovery. Each Azure region has a defined paired region within the same geopolitical boundary for GRS. For example, West US is paired with East US. This has a small impact on scalability targets for the storage account. The GRS copies in the paired region are not accessible to you, and GRS is best viewed as disaster recovery for Microsoft rather than for you. In the event of a major failure in the primary region, Microsoft would make the GRS replicas available, but this has never happened to date.

- Read-Access Geo-Redundant Storage (RA-GRS) This is GRS plus the ability to read the data in the secondary region, which makes it suitable for partial customer disaster recovery. If there is a problem with the primary region, you can change your application to have read-only access to the paired region. The storage client library supports a fallback mechanism via
- Microsoft.WindowsAzure.Storage.RetryPolicies.LocationMode to try to read from the secondary
copy if the primary copy can't be reached. This feature is built in for you. Your customers might not be able to perform updates, but at least the data is still available for viewing, reporting, etc.

  You also can use this if you have an application in which only a few users can write to the data but many people read the data. You can point your application that writes the data to the primary region but have the people only reading the data access the paired region. This is a good way to spread out the performance when accessing a storage account.

- Zone-Redundant Storage (ZRS) This option can only be used for block blobs in a standard storage account. It replicates your data across two to three facilities, either within a single region or across two regions. This provides higher durability than LRS, but ZRS accounts do not have metrics or logging capability.

## SECURITY AND AZURE STORAGE

Azure Storage provides a set of security features that help developers build secure applications. You can secure your storage account by using Role-Based Access Control (RBAC) and Microsoft Azure Active Directory (Azure AD). You can use client-side encryption, HTTPS, or SMB 3.0 to secure your data in transit. You can enable Storage Service Encryption, and the Azure Storage service will encrypt data written to the storage account. OS and Data disks for VMs now have Azure Disk Encryption that can be enabled. And secure access to the data plane objects (such as blobs) can be granted using a shared access signature (SAS). Let's talk a little more about each of these.

## SECURING YOUR STORAGE ACCOUNT

The first thing to think about is securing your storage account.

## STORAGE ACCOUNT KEYS

Each storage account has two authentication keys—a primary and a secondary—either of which can be used for any operation. There are two keys to allow occasional rollover of the keys to enhance security. It is critical that these keys be kept secure because their possession, along with the account name, allows unlimited access to any data in the storage account.

Say you're using key 1 for your storage account in multiple applications. You can regenerate key 2 and then change all the applications to use key 2, test them, and deploy them to production. Then, you can regenerate key 1, which removes access from anybody who is still using it. A good example of when you might want to do this is if your team uses a storage explorer that retains the storage account keys, and someone leaves the team or the company—you don't want them to have access to your data after they leaves. This can happen without a lot of notice, so you should have a procedure in place to know all the apps that need to change, and then practice rotating keys on a regular basis so that it's simple and not a big problem when it is necessary to rotate the keys in a hurry.

## USING RBAC, AZURE AD, AND AZURE KEY VAULT TO CONTROL ACCESS TO RESOURCE MANAGER STORAGE ACCOUNTS

RBAC and Azure AD With Resource Manager RBAC, you can assign roles to users, groups, or applications. The roles are tied to a specific set of actions that are allowed or disallowed. Using RBAC to grant access to a storage account only handles the management operations for that storage account. You can't use RBAC to grant access to objects in the data plane like a specific container or file share. You can, however, use RBAC to grant access to the storage account keys, which can then be used to read the data objects.

For example, you might grant someone the Owner role to the storage account. This means they can access the keys and thus the data objects, and they can create storage accounts and do pretty much anything.

You might grant someone else the Reader role. This allows them to read information about the storage account. They can read resource groups and resources, but they can't access the storage account keys and therefore can't access the data objects.

If someone is going to create VMs, you must grant them the Virtual Machine Contributor role, which grants them access to retrieve the storage account keys but not to create storage accounts. They need the keys to create the VHD files that are used for the VM disks.

Azure Key Vault Azure Key Vault helps safeguard cryptographic keys and secrets used by Azure applications and services. You could store your storage account keys in an Azure Key Vault. What does this do for you? While you can't control access to the data objects directly using Active Directory, you can control access to an Azure Key Vault using Active Directory. This means you can put your storage account keys in Azure Key Vault and then grant access to them for a specific user, group, or application.

Let's say you have an application running as a Web App that uploads files to a storage account. You want to be really sure nobody else can access those files. You add the application to Azure Active Directory and grant it access to the Azure Key Vault with that storage account's keys in it. After that, only that application can access those keys. This is much more secure than putting the keys in the *web.config* file where a hacker could get to them.

## SECURING ACCESS TO YOUR DATA

There are two ways to secure access to your data objects. We just talked about the first one—by controlling access to the storage account keys.

The second way to secure access is by using shared access signatures and stored access policies. A shared access signature (SAS) is a string containing a security token that can be attached to the URI for an asset that allows you to delegate access to specific storage objects and to specify constraints such as permissions and the date/time range of access.

You can grant access to blobs, containers, queue messages, files, and tables. With tables, you can grant access to specific partition keys. For example, if you were using geographical state for your partition key, you could give someone access to just the data for California.

You can fine-tune this by using a separation of concerns. You can give a web application permission to write messages to a queue, but not to read them or delete them. Then, you can give the worker role or Azure WebJob the permission to read the messages, process the messages, and delete the messages. Each component has the least amount of security required to do its job.

Here's an example of an SAS, with each parameter explained: http://mystorage.blob.core.windows.net/mycontainer/myblob.txt (URL to the blob)

?sv=2015-04-05 (storage service version)

&st=2015-12-10T22%3A18%3A26Z (start time, in UTC time and URL encoded)

&se=2015-12-10T22%3A23%3A26Z (end time, in UTC time and URL encoded)

&sr=b (resource is a blob)

&sp=r (read access)

&sip=168.1.5.60-168.1.5.70 (requests can only come from this range of IP addresses)

&spr=https (only allow HTTPS requests)

&sig=Z%2FRHIX5XcgOMq2rqI3OlWTjEg2tYkboXr1P9ZUXDtkk%3D (signature used for the authentication of the SAS)

Note that the SAS query parameters must be URL encoded, such as %3A for colon (:) and %20 for a space. This SAS gives read access to a blob from 12/10/2015 10:18 PM to 12/10/2015 10:23 PM.

When the storage service receives this request, it will take the query parameters and create the &sig value on its own and compare it to the one provided here. If they agree, it will verify the rest of the request. If our URL pointed to a file on a file share instead of a blob, the request would fail because blob is specified. If the request were to update the blob, it would fail because only read access has been granted.

132 of

There are both account-level SAS and service-level SAS. With account-level SAS, you can do things like list containers, create containers, delete file shares, and so on. With service-level SAS, you can only access the data objects. For example, you can upload a blob into a container.

You can also create stored access policies on container-like objects such as blob containers and file shares. This will let you set the default values for the query parameters, and then you can create the SAS by specifying the policy and the query parameter that is different for each request. For example, you might set up a policy that gives read access to a specific container. Then, when someone requests access to that container, you create an SAS from the policy and use it.

There are two advantages to using stored access policies. First, this hides the parameters that are defined in the policy. So if you set your policy to give access to 30 minutes, it won't show that in the URL—it just shows the policy name. This is more secure than letting all of your parameters be seen.

The second reason to use stored access policies is that they can be revoked. You can either change the expiration date to be prior to the current date/time or remove the policy altogether. You might do this if you accidentally provided access to an object you didn't mean to. With an ad hoc SAS URL, you have to remove the asset or change the storage account keys to revoke access.

Shared access signatures and stored access policies are the two most secure ways to provide access to your data objects.

## SECURING YOUR DATA IN TRANSIT

Another consideration when storing your data in Azure Storage is securing the data when it is being transferred between the storage service and your applications.

First, you should always use the HTTPS protocol, which ensures secure communication over the public Internet. Note that if you are using SAS, there is a query parameter that can be used that specifies that only the HTTPS protocol can be used with that URL.

For Azure File shares, SMB 3.0 running on Windows encrypts the data going across the public Internet. When Apple and Linux add security support to SMB 3.0, you will be able to mount file shares on those machines and have encrypted data in transit.

Last, you can use the client-side encryption feature of the .NET and Java storage client libraries to encrypt your data before sending it

133

across the wire. When you retrieve the data, you can then unencrypt it. This is built in to the storage client libraries for .NET and Java. This also counts as encryption at rest because the data is encrypted when stored.

## ENCRYPTION AT REST

Let's look at the various options available to encrypt the stored data.

## STORAGE SERVICE ENCRYPTION (SSE)

This is a new feature currently in preview. This lets you ask the storage service to encrypt blob data when writing it to Azure Storage. This feature has been requested by many companies to fulfill security and compliance requirements. It enables you to secure your data without having to add any code to any of your applications. Note that it only works for blob storage; tables, queues, and files will be unaffected.

This feature is per-storage account, and it can be enabled and disabled using the Azure portal, PowerShell, the CLI, the Azure Storage Resource Provider REST API, or the .NET storage client library. The keys are generated and managed by Microsoft at this time, but in the future you will get the ability to manage your own encryption keys.

This can be used with both Standard and Premium storage, but only with the new Resource Manager accounts. During the preview, you have to create a new storage account to try out this feature.

One thing to note: after being enabled, the service encrypts data written to the storage account. Any data already written to the account is not encrypted. If you later disable the encryption, any future data will not be encrypted, but it does retain encryption on the data written while encryption was enabled.

If you create a VM using an image from the Azure Marketplace, Azure performs a shallow copy of the image to your storage account in Azure Storage, and it is not encrypted even if you have SSE enabled. After it creates the VM and starts updating the image, SSE will start encrypting the data. For this reason, Microsoft recommends that you use Azure Disk Encryption on VMs created from images in the Azure Marketplace if you want them fully encrypted.

# AZURE DISK ENCRYPTION

This is another new feature that is currently in preview. This feature allows you to specify that the OS and data disks used by an IaaS VM should be encrypted. For Windows, the drives are encrypted with industry-standard BitLocker encryption technology. For Linux, encryption is performed using DMCrypt.

> Note For Linux VMs already running in Azure or new Linux VMs created from images in the Azure

> Marketplace, encryption of the OS disk is not currently supported. Encryption of the OS volume for Linux VMs is supported only for VMs that were encrypted on-premises and uploaded to Azure. This restriction only applies to the OS disk; encryption of data volumes for a Linux VM is supported.

Azure Disk Encryption is integrated with Azure Key Vault to allow you to control and manage the disk encryption keys.

Unlike SSE, when you enable this, it encrypts the whole disk, including data that was previously written. You can bring your own encrypted images into Azure and upload them and store the keys in Azure Key Vault, and the image will continue to be encrypted. You can also upload an image that is not encrypted or create a VM from the Azure Gallery and ask that its disks be encrypted.

This is the method recommended by Microsoft to encrypt your IaaS VMs at rest. Note that if you turn on both SSE and Azure Disk Encryption, it will work fine. Your data will simply be double-encrypted.

# CLIENT-SIDE ENCRYPTION

We looked at client-side encryption when discussing encryption in transit. The data is encrypted by the application and sent across the wire to be stored in the storage account. When retrieved, the data is decrypted by the application. Because the data is stored encrypted, this is encryption at rest.

For this encryption, you can encrypt the data in blobs, tables, and queues, rather than just blobs like

SSE. Also, you can bring your own keys or use keys generated by Microsoft. If you store your encryption keys in Azure Key Vault, you can use Azure Active Directory to specifically grant access to the keys.

This allows you to control who can read the vault and retrieve the keys being used for clientside encryption.

This is the most secure method of encrypting your data, but it does require that you add code to perform the encryption and decryption. If you only have blobs that need to be encrypted, you may choose to use a combination of HTTPS and SSE to meet the requirement that your data be encrypted at rest.

## USING STORAGE ANALYTICS TO AUDIT ACCESS

You may want to see how people are accessing your storage account. Do all the requests use an SAS? How many people are accessing the storage account using the actual storage account keys?

To check this, you can enable the logging in the Azure Storage Analytics and check the results after a while. Enabling the logging tells the Azure Storage service to log all requests to the storage account. (Note that at this time, only blobs, tables, and queues are supported.)

The logs are stored in a container called $logs in blob storage. They are stored by date and time, collected by hour. If there is no activity, no logs are generated.

Here are the fields that are stored in the logs.

<version-number>;<request-start-time>;<operation-type>;<request-status>;<http-statuscode>;<end-to-end-latency-in-ms>;<server-latency-in-ms>;<authentication-type>;<requesteraccount-name>;<owner-account-name>;<service-type>;<request-url>;<requested-objectkey>;<request-id-header>;<operation-count>;<requester-ip-address>;<request-versionheader>;<request-header-size>;<request-packet-size>;<response-header-size>;<response-packetsize>;<request-content-length>;<request-md5>;<server-md5>;<etag-identifier>;<last-modifiedtime>;<conditions-used>;<user-agent-header>;<referrer-header>;<client-request-id>

The fields in bold are the ones in which we are interested. So if you look at a log file, these are the three cases we can look for:

1. The blob is public, and it is accessed using a URL without an SAS. In this case, the request-status will be *AnonymousSuccess* and the authentication type will be *anonymous*.

   1.0;2015-11-

17T02:01:29.0488963Z;GetBlob;AnonymousSuccess;200;12
4;37;anonymous;;mystorage...

2. The blob is private and was used with an SAS. In this case,
   the request-status is *SASSuccess* and the authentication type
   is *sas*.

   1.0;2015-11-
   16T18:30:05.6556115Z;GetBlob;SASSuccess;200;416;64;sa
   s;;mystorage...

3. The blob is private, and the storage key was used to access
   it. In this case, the request-status is *Success* and the
   authentication type is *authenticated*.

   1.0;2015-11-
   16T18:32:24.3174537Z;GetBlob;Success;206;59;22;authent
   icated;mystorage...

To view and analyze these log files, you can use the Microsoft Message
Analyzer (free from Microsoft).

You can download the Message Analyzer here:

https://www.microsoft.com/download/details.aspx?id=44226.         The
operating                 guide                 is                 here:
https://technet.microsoft.com/library/jj649776.aspx.

The Message Analyzer lets you search and filter the data. An example
of when you might want to do this is if you have your keys stored in
Azure Key Vault and only one application has access to the Azure Key
Vault. In that case, you might search for instances where *GetBlob* was
called and make sure there aren't any calls that were authenticated in
any other way.

Important For Azure Analytics, the metrics tables start with $metrics,
and the logs container in blob storage is called $logs. You cannot even
see the tables and container using PowerShell, the Visual Studio Cloud
Explorer, or the Azure portal.

You can see the tables and container and even open and view the
entities and blobs using the

Microsoft Azure Storage Explorer (http://storageexplorer.com). The
Cerebrata Azure Management Studio and Cloud Portam allow you to
access and view these objects (http://www.cerebrata.com) as well.

You can also write your own code using one of the storage client
libraries to retrieve the data from table storage and blob storage.
Other storage explorers listed in the article at the beginning of this
chapter may also enable you to view this data.

# USING CROSS-ORIGIN RESOURCE SHARING (CORS)

When a web browser running in one domain makes an HTTP request for a resource in another domain, it's called a cross-origin HTTP request. If the request is made in a script language such as JavaScript, the browser will not allow the request.

For example, if a web application running on contoso.com makes a request for a jpeg on fabrikam.blob.core.windows.net, it will be blocked.

What if you actually *want* to share the images in your storage account with Contoso? Azure Storage allows you to enable CORS—Cross-Origin Resource Sharing. For this example, you would enable CORS on the fabrikam storage account and allow access from contoso.com. You can do this by using the Rest API or the storage client library.

# CREATING AND MANAGING STORAGE

In this section, we are going to go through several exercises to show the different ways you can access your data objects. First, we'll use the Azure portal and the Visual Studio Cloud Explorer, then we'll do some of the same operations using PowerShell. Here's what we'll do:

- Create a storage account using the Azure portal.

- Create a blob container and upload blobs using the Visual Studio Cloud Explorer.

- Create a file share and upload files using the Azure portal.

- Create a table and add records to it using Visual Studio Cloud Explorer.

- Create a storage account using Azure PowerShell.

- Create a blob container and upload blobs using PowerShell.

- Create a file share and upload files using PowerShell.

- To do the Azure PowerShell demos, you need to install Azure PowerShell.

# CREATE A STORAGE ACCOUNT USING THE AZURE PORTAL

To create a storage account, log into the Azure portal. Click New > Data + Storage > Storage Account. You see a screen similar to Figure 4-1.

1. First, fill in a name for the storage account. The name must be globally unique because it is used as part of the URL. This will be used in the endpoints for blobs, files, tables, and queues. In Figure 4-1, the storage account name is azurebooktest. This means the blobs (for example) will be addressable as http://azurebooktest.blob.core.windows.net.

2. The next field displayed is the Deployment Model. You want to create a Resource Manager storage account, so select Resource Manager.

3. Account Kind can be General Purpose or Blob Storage. Select General Purpose so you can use the same account for blobs, files, and tables.

4. For Replication, the default is GRS—Globally Redundant Storage. Change this to LRS (Locally Redundant Storage), which has the lowest cost. For test data, you don't need it to be replicated in a completely different region.

5. If you manage multiple subscriptions, select the one you want to be used for this storage account.

6. For Resource Group, let's create a new one just for this chapter. Specify the name of the resource group. In Figure 4-1, the resource group is called azurebookch4rg.

7. For Location, select the Azure region closest to you for the best performance.

8. Select the Pin To Dashboard check box and click Create. Azure will provision the storage account and add it to the Dashboard.

   Now that you've created a Resource Manager storage account in its own resource group, let's take a look at it.

9. If your storage account wasn't automatically displayed after being created, click your new storage account from the

Dashboard. A blade will be displayed with information about your storage account (Figure 4-2).

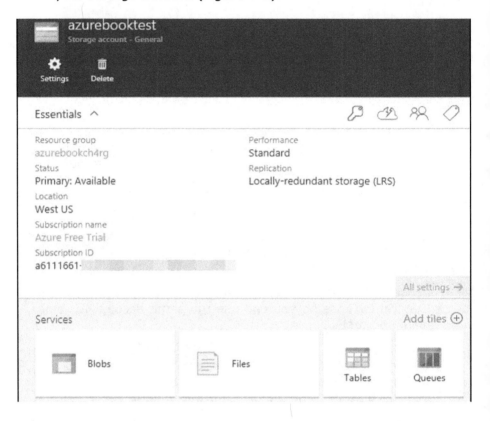

Figure 4-2 View your new storage account.

10. Click All Settings to bring up the Settings blade (Figure 4-3).

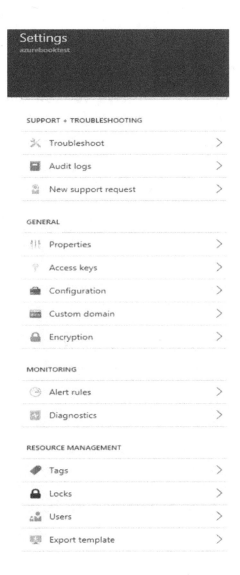

Figure 4-3 Settings blade for the new storage account.

Here are some of the options in the Settings blade:

- Access Keys This shows you your storage account name and

  the two access keys. From the Access Keys blade, you can copy any of the values to the Windows clipboard. You can also regenerate the storage account access keys here.

- Configuration This allows you to change the replication. Yours is LRS if that's what you selected when creating the storage account. You can change it here to GRS or RA-GRS.

- Custom Domain This is where you can configure a custom domain for your storage account. For example, rather than calling it robinscompany.blob.core.windows.net, you can assign a domain to it and refer to it as storage.robinscompany.com.

- Encryption This is where you can sign up for the Storage Service Encryption preview. At some point, this will be where you enable and disable SSE for the storage account.

- Diagnostics This is where you can turn on the Storage Analytics and the logging.

- Users This is where you can grant management-plane access for this specific storage account.

## CREATE A CONTAINER AND UPLOAD BLOBS USING VISUAL STUDIO CLOUD EXPLORER

Now you want to create a container and upload some files to it using Visual Studio Cloud Explorer.

1. Run Visual Studio. If you don't have the Azure Tools installed, you can use the Web Platform Installer to install them.

2. Click View > Cloud Explorer. You see a screen like the one in Figure 4-4.

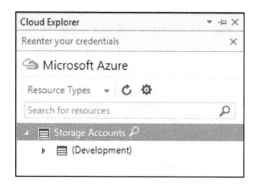

Figure 4-4 Cloud Explorer.

3. Click the Settings icon to get to the login screen (Figure 4-5).

Figure 4-5 Select the Azure account with which to log into the Cloud Explorer.

If you don't have any Azure accounts displayed in the list, click the drop-down list and select Add An Account. If you do have accounts displayed, select the one you want to use and log into it. Click Apply. After logging in, you see something like Figure 4-6.

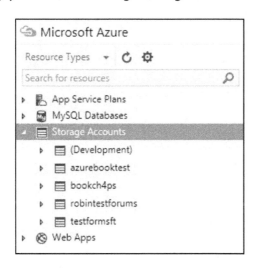

Figure 4-6 Visual Studio Cloud Explorer, showing resources.

4. Open the storage account you created with the portal. In the example, that's azurebooktest. The storage account has Blob

Containers, Queues, and Tables. Right-click Blob Containers and select Create Blob Container, as displayed in Figure 4-7.

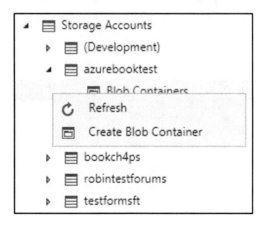

Figure 4-7 Create blob container.

5. It shows a text box; type in the container name. The example uses test-vs. Press Enter; now it shows your new container under Blob Containers. Double-click the container name to open a screen where you can upload blobs (Figure 4-8).

Figure 4-8 Ready to upload blobs into the container.

6. To upload blobs into the container, click the icon on the top row next to the filter that shows an up arrow with a line over it (this is the same icon used in Figure 4-14). The Upload New File dialog opens (Figure 4-9). Browse to find a file. You

can set a folder name here. Note that this is the pseudo-foldering discussed earlier—it includes the folder name in the blob name with a forward slash. If you leave the folder blank, it will put the file in the root of the container.

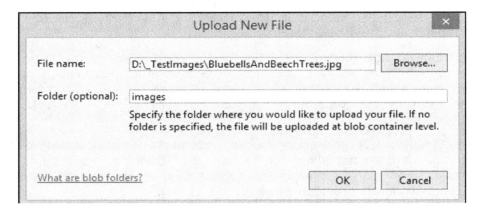

Figure 4-9 Dialog for uploading blobs into the container.

7. Upload some files into the root and some files into a folder. You should see something similar to Figure 4-10. This figure shows a folder called images and two blobs in the root. Note that it shows the URL to the blobs. If you open the images folder, it will show the blobs there, and all of the URLs will have /images/ in them.

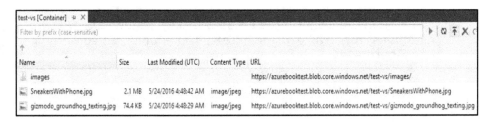

Figure 4-10 Screen showing blobs uploaded into the container.

8. You can delete blobs from the container by using the red X icon, and you can download blobs and view them in the picture viewer by double-clicking the entry in the table or by clicking the forward arrow icon.

One thing this tool does not allow you to do is set the Access Type of the container. By default, the Cloud Explorer sets it to Private. The Access Type defines who can access the blobs and the container. If this is Private, the container and the blobs in the container can only be accessed by someone who has the account credentials (account name and key) or a URL that includes an SAS. If you set this to Blob, then anyone with a URL can view the associated blob but cannot view the container properties and metadata or the list of blobs in the container. If you set this to Container, then everyone has read access to the container and the blobs therein.

You can change this in the Azure portal and through some storage explorers. In the Azure portal, go to the storage account, click Blobs, and then select the container. A blade will open on the right showing the blobs in the container. Click Access Policy to set it to Blob or Public.

The Cloud Explorer is a pretty simple implementation of accessing blob storage. It does not allow you to upload or download folders full of images. For more sophisticated applications, check out the list of storage explorers provided earlier in this section.

## CREATE A FILE SHARE AND UPLOAD FILES USING THE AZURE PORTAL

In this section, you will create an Azure File share and then upload some files to it. For this demo, you'll use the Azure portal. You can't use the Cloud Explorer in Visual Studio because it doesn't support Azure Files.

1. Log into the Azure portal. Click All Resources and then select the storage account you created using the portal. In the examples, this was azurebooktest. You should see something like Figure 411.

Figure 4-11 View storage account.

2. Click Files to open the File Service blade shown in Figure 4-12.

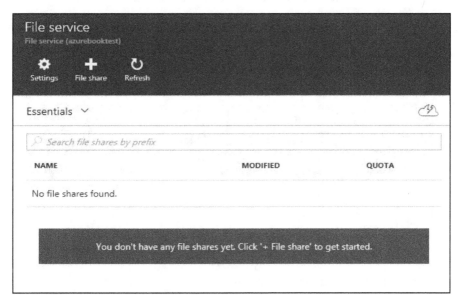

Figure 4-12 File Service blade.

3. You don't have any file shares yet. Create one by clicking File Share. This will show the New File Share blade (Figure 4-13).

147

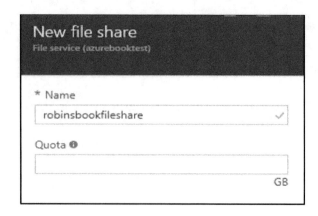

Figure 4-13 Create a new file share.

4. Provide a name for the file share. If you want the maximum size of the file share to be less than the allowed 5,120 GB, specify the desired value in the Quota field. To maximize the size of the file share, leave the Quota blank.

   Click Create at the bottom of the blade, and Azure will create the file share for you and display it in the File Service blade.

5. Click the new file share to bring up the file share's blade. You see something like Figure 4-14.

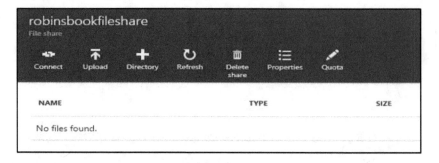

Figure 4-14 Create a new file share.

Let's look at what the icons do.

- Connect This gives you the NET USE statement that you can use in a command window to map the network share to a local drive letter.

- Upload This allows you to upload files.

- Directory This lets you create a directory in the folder currently displayed. For you, that's the root folder.

- Refresh This refreshes the displayed information.

- Delete share This will delete the file share and all the files on it.

- Properties This shows the Properties blade for the file share. This shows the name, URL, quota, usage, and so on.

- Quota This lets you modify the quota specified.

Now upload some files. Click the Upload icon to show the Upload Files blade (Figure 4-15).

Figure 4-15 The Upload Files blade.

6. Click the file folder icon. In the Choose File To Upload dialog that displays, browse to any folder and select some files to upload. You can upload up to four files at a time. If you select more than four, it will ignore the extras. After selecting them and returning to the Upload Files blade, it shows the files in a list. Click the Start Upload button displayed in Figure 4-16 to upload the files.

Figure 4-16 Uploading files.

The portal will show the progress while uploading the files and then show the files in the File Share blade, as illustrated in Figure 4-17.

| NAME | TYPE | SIZE | |
|------|------|------|---|
| BluebellsAndBeechTrees.jpg | File | 1.34 MB | ... |
| bravia_bench_paint.bmp | File | 3.75 MB | ... |
| Chihuly.jpg | File | 5.49 MB | ... |
| GuyEyeingOreos.png | File | 163.54 KB | ... |

**robinsbookfileshare**
File share

Connect | Upload | Directory | Refresh | Delete share | Properties | Quota

Figure 4-17 Uploaded files.

# CREATE A TABLE AND ADD RECORDS USING THE VISUAL STUDIO CLOUD EXPLORER

Now you can create a table in your storage account and add some entities to it. You can use one of the storage explorer tools mentioned earlier in this book, but let's see how easy it is to use the Visual Studio Cloud Explorer to do this task.

If you've done the steps in the last section that showed how to use the Cloud Explorer to add blobs to blob storage, this will be just as easy. If you don't still have the Cloud Explorer open, open it again and log in to your Azure account again.

In Cloud Explorer, right-click Tables and select Create Table. You will be prompted for the name of the table, which must be unique within your storage account. After pressing Enter to create the new table, double-click the table name to see something similar to Figure 4-18.

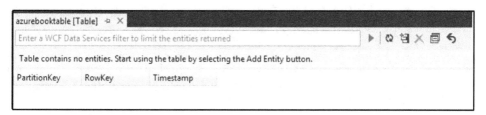

Figure 4-18 Editing a new table.

You don't have any entities, so add one by clicking the icon with the + in it.

As discussed in the section "Table storage" earlier in this chapter, you have to think about what you want to use for PartitionKey and RowKey to get the best performance.

For this example, use geographic state abbreviation for the PartitionKey and city name for the RowKey. For properties, add Population as Int32 and LandArea as a Double. Fill in values for each of the fields. Figure 4-19 shows what the entity looks like before adding it to the table.

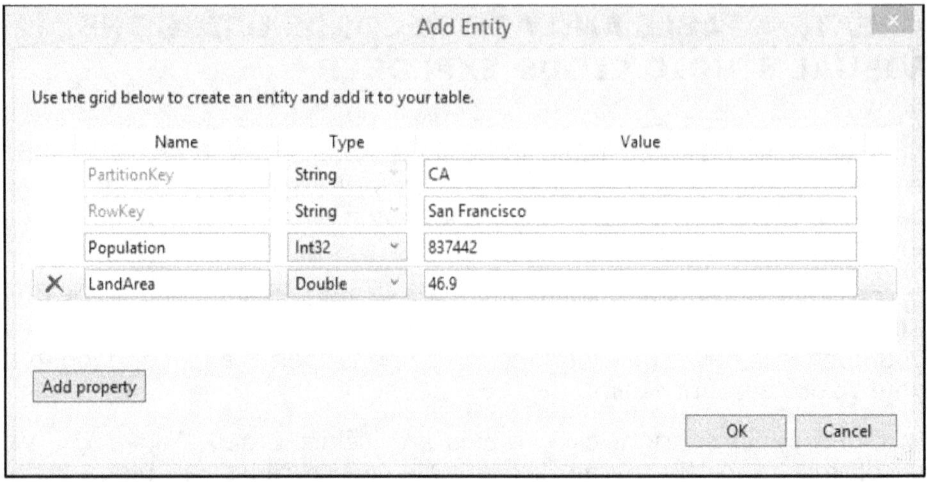

**Add Entity** ✕

Use the grid below to create an entity and add it to your table.

| Name | Type | Value |
|------|------|-------|
| PartitionKey | String | CA |
| RowKey | String | San Francisco |
| Population | Int32 | 837442 |
| ✕ LandArea | Double | 46.9 |

Add property

OK    Cancel

Figure 4-19 Add an entity to the table.

Click OK to save the entity. Add another entity, and this time, add another property besides

Population and LandArea, such as GPSCoordinates. Add a couple more entities, including whatever properties you want. If you want to edit an entity after saving it, you can right-click the entity and select Edit. You also can delete entities using this view.

After entering a few entities, you should have something similar to Figure 4-20.

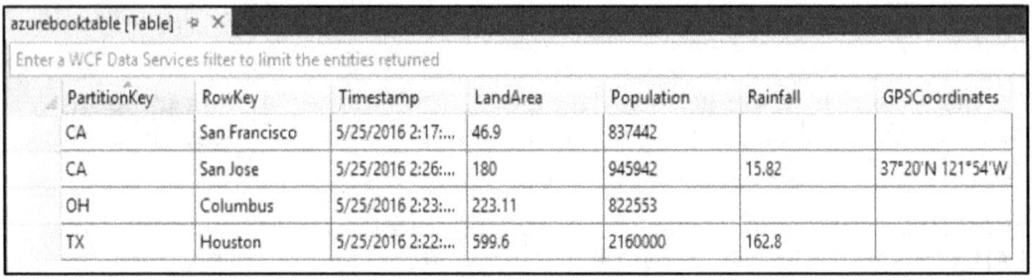

azurebooktable [Table]  ⊉  ✕

Enter a WCF Data Services filter to limit the entities returned

| PartitionKey | RowKey | Timestamp | LandArea | Population | Rainfall | GPSCoordinates |
|--------------|--------|-----------|----------|-----------|----------|----------------|
| CA | San Francisco | 5/25/2016 2:17:... | 46.9 | 837442 | | |
| CA | San Jose | 5/25/2016 2:26:... | 180 | 945942 | 15.82 | 37°20'N 121°54'W |
| OH | Columbus | 5/25/2016 2:23:... | 223.11 | 822553 | | |
| TX | Houston | 5/25/2016 2:22:... | 599.6 | 2160000 | 162.8 | |

Figure 4-20 View the table after adding entities.

You can see the PartitionKey and RowKey combination is unique for all of the entities. The rest of each row in the table is the list of key/value pairs. Not all entities have the same properties. The entity for

San Francisco only has LandArea and Population; the entity for San Jose is the only one with GPSCoordinates. This is a strength of Azure Tables—the key/value pairs can vary for each entity.

You can create tables by using a designer such as this one in Visual Studio, but for adding, changing, and deleting entities in an application, you will probably want to write your own code using the storage client library. For examples, please check out this link: http://azure.microsoft.com/ documentation/articles/storage-dotnet-how-to-use-tables/.

## CREATE A STORAGE ACCOUNT USING POWERSHELL

Let's see how to do many of the same operations using Azure PowerShell cmdlets.

1. First, you need to run Azure PowerShell ISE.

2. Log into your Azure account using the PowerShell cmdlet *Login-AzureRmAccount*. You will be prompted for your Azure credentials; go ahead and log in.

   > Login-AzureRmAccount

   Note: There is also a cmdlet called *Add-AzureAccount*. This is for using classic resources. All of the cmdlets for Resource Manager accounts have "Rm" after the word "Azure" in the cmdlet.

   After logging into the account, it should show the subscription in the command window.

3. Now you need a resource group in which to put your storage account. Use the same one you created in the portal when you created the storage account there. If you put all of the resources created in this chapter in the same resource group, then at the end you can delete them in one fell swoop by deleting the resource group.

If you want to create a new resource group, you can do that with the *NewAzureRmResourceGroup* cmdlet like this:

> New-AzureRmResourceGroup "nameofgroup" –Location "location" An example of Location is West US.

You can retrieve a list of resource groups by using the *Get-AzureRmResourceGroup* cmdlet. When you run this, you see the resource group you set up when creating the storage account in the portal (Figure 4-21).

```
PS C:\Windows\system32> Get-AzureRmResourceGroup

ResourceGroupName  : azurebookch4rg
Location           : westus
ProvisioningState  : Succeeded
Tags               :
ResourceId         : /subscriptions/a6111661-            /resourceGroups/azure
                     bookch4rg
```

Figure 4-21 Show available resource groups.

4.  Now let's create the storage account. You want to create a Resource Manager storage account and specify the resource group. You also specify the storage account name, the location, and the type, which is for the redundancy type. You want to use locally redundant storage for the same reasons mentioned when creating the storage account using the Azure portal. Select your own storage account name. Here's what the command looks like:

>    New-AzureRmStorageAccount    –ResourceGroup "bookch4rg" –StorageAccountName "bookch4ps" –Location "West US" –Type "Standard_LRS"

For a full list of locations, you can run the PowerShell cmdlet *Get-AzureRmLocation*.

Fill in your own values, and when you're ready, press Enter to execute the command. It will take a couple of minutes. When it's done, it will show you your new storage account. It should look like Figure 4-22.

```
ResourceGroupName   : azurebookch4rg
StorageAccountName  : bookch4ps
Id                  : /subscriptions/a6111661-2ef9-            /resourceGroups/azu
                      rebookch4rg/providers/Microsoft.Storage/storageAccounts/bookch4ps
Location            : westus
AccountType         : StandardLRS
CreationTime        : 5/23/2016 12:55:28 AM
CustomDomain        :
LastGeoFailoverTime :
PrimaryEndpoints    : Microsoft.Azure.Management.Storage.Models.Endpoints
PrimaryLocation     : westus
ProvisioningState   : Succeeded
SecondaryEndpoints  :
SecondaryLocation   :
StatusOfPrimary     : Available
StatusOfSecondary   :
Tags                : {}
Context             : Microsoft.WindowsAzure.Commands.Common.Storage.AzureStorageContext
```

Figure 4-22 The PowerShell output from creating the storage account.

154

If you log into the Azure portal, you can see your new resource group and the new storage account in the resource group.

## CREATE A CONTAINER AND UPLOAD BLOBS USING POWERSHELL

Now you'll create a container and upload some blobs. In the example, the test files are in D:\_TestImages. That path is used when uploading those files to Blob storage.

Note These cmdlets are Azure Storage data-plane cmdlets, not Azure Service Management (ASM) or Azure Resource Manager cmdlets, which are management-plane cmdlets. The cmdlet to create a storage account is a management-plane cmdlet. These data-plane cmdlets can be used with both ASM and Resource Manager storage accounts.

If you're not running the PowerShell ISE and are logged into your Azure account, do that now. You're going to create a script that you can save and use later. In addition to the path to your local pictures, you will need the name and access key of your storage account.

1. Set up variable names for the storage account name and key—*$StorageAccountName* and *$StorageAccountKey*. Fill in your storage account name and key here.

   $StorageAccountName = "yourStorageAccountName"

   $StorageAccountKey = "yourStorageAccountKey"

2. Next, you'll define the storage account context using the storage account name and key. You will use this context for authentication with subsequent commands against the storage account. This is easier (and safer) than specifying the storage account name and key all the time.

$ctx      =      New-AzureStorageContext      -StorageAccountName $StorageAccountName `

   -StorageAccountKey $StorageAccountKey

   Note that there is a continuation character (the backward tick mark) at the end of the first line.

3. Next, you'll add a variable for the name of your container, then you'll create the container. The example uses *test-ps*.

   $ContainerName = "test-ps"

155

#create a new container with public access to the blobs

New-AzureStorageContainer  -Name  $ContainerName  -Context $ctx -Permission Blob

This creates a container in your storage account (as defined by the context) with a permission of Blob, which means the blobs can be accessed on the Internet with a URL.

4. Now you need to set a variable pointing at the local directory with the images. You can upload any files, just remember the larger they are, the longer it will take to upload! Using a variable here makes it easier to change it later in case you use this in multiple places.

$localFileDirectory = "D:\_TestImages\"

5. Now you can upload a blob. First, you'll set a variable name for the blob name to be the same as the file name. Then, append it to the *$localFileDirectory* variable. The file will be uploaded from the local disk to the specified container.

$BlobName = "SnowyCabin.jpg"

$localFile = $localFileDirectory + $BlobName

Set-AzureStorageBlobContent  -File  $localFile  -Container $ContainerName `

  -Blob $BlobName -Context $ctx

To run the script, press F5. To run parts of the script, highlight the bits you want to run and press F8 (or click the Run Selection icon). If you have to run this repeatedly, you only want to create the container once, so once that's successful, only select commands starting after that. When you run this and upload the file, you get back verification in the command window (Figure 4-23).

```
PS C:\Windows\system32> Set-AzureStorageBlobContent -File $localFile -Container $ContainerName
    -Blob $BlobName -Context $ctx


    Container Uri: https://bookch4ps.blob.core.windows.net/test-vs

Name              BlobType    Length      ContentType       LastModified      SnapshotTime
----              --------    ------      -----------       ------------      ------------
SnowyCabin.jpg    BlockBlob   184108                        application/...   5/24/2016 5:...
```

Figure 4-23 Upload file to blob storage.

6. To upload more files, copy and paste the three lines of PowerShell, changing the *$BlobName* variable for each set you paste.

7. After uploading some files, you can list them by using the *Get-AzureStorageBlob* PowerShell cmdlet.

    # get list of blobs and see the new one has been added to the container

    Get-AzureStorageBlob -Container $ContainerName -Context $ctx

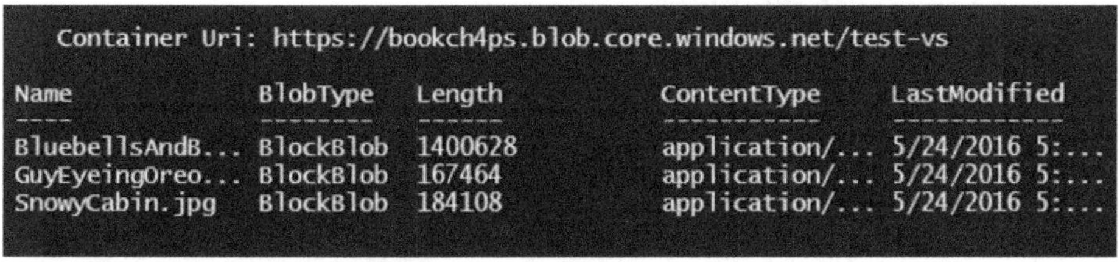

```
Container Uri: https://bookch4ps.blob.core.windows.net/test-vs

Name              BlobType    Length     ContentType      LastModified
----              --------    ------     -----------      ------------
BluebellsAndB...  BlockBlob   1400628    application/...  5/24/2016 5:...
GuyEyeingOreo...  BlockBlob   167464     application/...  5/24/2016 5:...
SnowyCabin.jpg    BlockBlob   184108     application/...  5/24/2016 5:...
```

Figure 4-24 List of files uploaded to blob storage.

You can also see the container and blobs if you log into the Azure portal and go to the storage account.

There are also PowerShell commands for downloading blobs, deleting blobs, copying blobs, etc.

## CREATE A FILE SHARE AND UPLOAD FILES USING POWERSHELL

Now you're going to create a file share in the storage account and upload some files to it using PowerShell. This is very similar to the PowerShell for uploading blobs.

In our example, the storage account is called bookch4ps; the test files are in D:\_TestImages. That path is needed when uploading those files to File storage.

If needed, run the PowerShell ISE and log into your Azure account. You're going to create a script that you can save and use later. In addition to the path to your local pictures, you will need the name and access key of your storage account.

1. Set up variable names for the storage account name and key: *$StorageAccountName* and *$StorageAccountKey*. Fill in your storage account name and key.

   $StorageAccountName = "yourStorageAccountName"

   $StorageAccountKey = "yourStorageAccountKey"

2. Next, you'll define the storage account context using the storage account name and key. You will use this context for authentication with subsequent commands against the storage account. This is easier (and safer) than specifying the storage account name and key all the time.

   $ctx = New-AzureStorageContext -StorageAccountName $StorageAccountName `

      -StorageAccountKey $StorageAccountKey

   Note that there is a continuation character at the end of the first line—the backward tick mark.

3. Now you'll set the variable for the name of the file share to whatever you like; the example will use *psfileshare*. Then, you'll create the new file share, assigning it to the variable *$s*.

   $shareName = "psfileshare"

   $s = New-AzureStorageShare $shareName -Context $ctx

4. Now set a variable for the local location of the files to be uploaded.

   $localFolderName = "D:\_TestImages\"

5. Now you can do the actual upload of the file. Set a variable for the file name, create the local path (directory + file name), and then use the PowerShell cmdlet *Set-AzureStorageFileContent* to upload the file.

   $fileName = "DogInCatTree.png"

   $localFile = $localFolderName + $fileName

   Set-AzureStorageFileContent -Share $s -Source $localFile -Path images

6. Copy this a couple of times and run it with different file names to upload multiple files. Now run the script and watch as it echoes the successful commands back to you.

7. You can call *Get-AzureStorageFile* to retrieve the list of files in the root of the file share.

Get-AzureStorageFile -Share $s

8. Figure 4-25 shows the output from the example.

```
PS C:\Users\robin> Get-AzureStorageFile -Share $s


   Directory: https://bookch4ps.file.core.windows.net/psfileshare

Type                         Length Name
----                         ------ ----
                                  1 BluebellsAndBeechTrees.jpg
                                  1 DogInCatTree.png
                                  1 SnowyCabin.jpg
```

Figure 4-25 Files uploaded to the file share.

There are also PowerShell commands for downloading files, deleting files, copying files, etc.

## AZCOPY: A VERY USEFUL TOOL

Before finishing the chapter on Azure Storage, you need to know about AzCopy. This is a free tool provided by the Azure Storage team to move data around. The core use case is asynchronous serverside copies. When you copy blobs or files from one storage account to another, they are not downloaded from the first storage account to your local machine and then uploaded to the second storage account. The blobs and files are copied directly within Azure.

Here are some of the things you can do with AzCopy:

- Upload blobs from the local folder on a machine to Azure Blob storage.

- Upload files from the local folder on a machine to Azure File storage.

- Copy blobs from one container to another in the same storage account.

- Copy blobs from one storage account to another, either in the same region or in a different region.

159

- Copy files from one file share to another in the same storage account.

- Copy files from one storage account to another, either in the same region or in a different region.

- Copy blobs from one storage account to an Azure File share in the same storage account or in a different storage account.

- Copy files from an Azure File share to a blob container in the same storage account or in a different storage account.

- Export a table to an output file in JSON or CSV format. You can export this to blob storage.

- Import the previously exported table data from a JSON file into a new table. (Note: It won't import from a CSV file.)

As you can see, there are a lot of possibilities when using AzCopy. It also has a bunch of options. For example, you can tell it to only copy data where the source files are newer than the target files. You can also have it copy data only where the source files are older than the target files. And you can combine these options to ask it to copy only files that don't exist in the destination at all.

AzCopy is frequently used to make backups of Azure Blob storage. Maybe you have files in Blob storage that are updated by your customer frequently, and you want a backup in case there's a problem. You can do something like this:

- Do a full backup on Saturday from the source container to a target container and put the date in the name of the target container.

- For each subsequent day, do an incremental copy—copy only the files that are newer in the source than in the destination.

If your customer uploads a file by mistake, if they contact you before end of day, you can retrieve the previous version from the backup copy.

Here are some other use cases:

- You want to move your data from a classic storage account to a Resource Manager storage account. You can do this by using AzCopy, and then you can change your applications to point to the data in the new location.

- You want to move your data from general-purpose storage to cool storage. You would copy your blobs from the general-purpose storage account to the new Blob storage account, then delete the blobs from the original location.

## THE AZURE DATA MOVEMENT LIBRARY

Many people wanted to be able to call AzCopy with their own specialized case. Because of this, the Azure Storage team open sourced the Azure Storage Data Movement Library, giving you programmatic access to AzCopy. For more information, check out the repository and samples on GitHub at https://github.com/Azure/azure-storage-net-data-movement.

www.ingramcontent.com/pod-product-compliance
Lightning Source LLC
La Vergne TN
LVHW051238050326
832903LV00028B/2463